FOR MISSIONARIES ONLY

Joseph L. Cannon

BAKER BOOK HOUSE • GRAND RAPIDS, MICHIGAN

Library of Congress Catalog Card Number: 70-89619

Paperback edition issued 1975
ISBN: 0-8010-2347-5

PHOTOLITHOPRINTED BY CUSHING - MALLOY, INC.
ANN ARBOR, MICHIGAN, UNITED STATES OF AMERICA
1975

Preface

Have I then become your enemy by telling you the truth? — GALATIANS 4:16

A good friend of mine asked me if I was referring to him in one of the sections of this book. It took me about fifteen minutes to say Yes. No rudeness was meant by me, and I have tried not to be offensive, but I find it hard to speak of specific problems in a general way. At the same time, if the reader is not helped in a definite and constructive way the purpose of the writing is frustrated. Quite a few of my fellow missionaries have read the manuscript, and I am indebted to them for their kind, but not always flattering comments. My sister, who pored over the manuscript fixing this and that, and straightening out my poor English (I hope she didn't miss anything), said that the contents of this little book would make some folks angry. I really don't know whether there will be enough interest in what I wrote for that to happen, but if it does, I hope it is not because of some discourtesy of mine, but because something true and worthwhile has stirred them up. Things that get under my skin bother me the most and benefit me the most. Maybe this is true of others also.

A friend told me the other day that he heard I had written a book on "missionary methods." I objected, stating that it was not my purpose to do so; nor do I feel qualified by study or experience to do so. This book was written with the idea of sharing with missionaries and those interested in missionary work some of my own feelings and experiences, hoping that there may be some encouragement, some blessing for those who read it.

A good brother accused me of "being on the defensive . . . speaking subjectively from your own limited experience." To this I must plead guilty; my only subjective defense being a heartfelt hope that maybe some missionary sweating it out somewhere in the world might find some beneficial thing in my obviously limited experience.

JOE CANNON

Contents

FOR MISSIONARIES ONLY

Introduction

In Retrospect

The years flash through my mind in kaleidoscopic scenes — great things, little things. I fall into fond reverie. With my heart flooded and torn by cross currents of fact and fantasy, and my mind colored by pride and prejudice, what can I write? What is important? From this carousel of mental images and cherished sounds what shall I choose? Ah, there are things about which I would like to boast. I could recommend myself and so betray the grace of Christ and fail to glorify God. I could choose the seeming meritorious deeds and let them represent the past and ignore the mountain of sins and errors that God has forgiven. Maybe I should write objectively and give a piercing, cold analysis of what I remember. I can't do that. I'm not that kind of guy. I feel fatherly about the work I have been involved in. I am subjective, defensive and selfish. I am sentimental about the past twenty years and any adverse criticism, true or false, makes me mad. I shall make some observations, but I am limited by my own ignorance, and I feel that only He who can see the end from the beginning can draw conclusions that are real.

Up and Down

The winds of change blow across the harvest fields and the golden grain blows this way and that. Up and down it moves in unpredictable ways. So it has been in Japan. There were periods of intense interest when dozens and dozens were reaped for Christ. It seemed as if we would sweep the whole city, the whole province, the whole nation. And then it was over. The wheat leaned away from the sickle and we missed. The school of fish moved on and the hooks were left dangling. We must search; we must sow again in hope of a future harvest. We are encouraged; we are discouraged. You hear how fruitful the work in Japan has been. You hear also how unfruitful it has been. Both reports are correct. To see one side and not the other is to settle for half the story. The ups and downs of this field require the hard work of the harvester in the field and the steady patience of a fisherman. I have learned that the watchword is faithfulness. Faithfulness through it all and in spite of it all.

Back and Forth

This has been the story of missionaries. Always the goings and comings. Where are my companions of former years? I search for their presence as for a happy dream that has slipped from remembrance. I have felt the loneliness of my vigil. Yet their work lives on in the lives of those they brought to Christ. The accumulative effect of missionary endeavor is worth it all. As the workers rotate the field is harvested. The price paid was high. It took its toll of health and wealth, suffering and scars. I rejoice with those who are carrying on, and I weep for the good men brought low. My missionary brethren made me sweet and made me bitter. They were saints; they were sinners. As I ponder the reasons for their comings and goings, I think, What if they had never come? There would be nothing in Japan now. There would not be scores of churches of Christ and the institutions of good works and glory to God. I am satisfied, I am thankful. Come and go, oh, missionary of Christ! Let the work go on!

In and Out

This was and is the story of Japanese Christians. Baptize ten, lose ten. Baptize ten, lose nine. Baptize ten, lose five. Baptize none and lose none. How hard it is for them to buck their pagan society. How great their tribulations have been! We can criticize, but can we understand? We can be disillusioned with them, but can we bear with them? Some of these children last about as long in the faith as their missionary fathers do in the field. They are as true to Christ as their teachers are to them. But alas, this is only partly true, for some leave sooner. But, thanks be to God, some never leave. I have been here long enough to see another phenomena — the return of the prodigal. What happy times these are, when the ghostly images of faces almost forgotten take concrete form again. The reasons for their disappearance are forgotten; only the joy of their return fills our hearts. Yes, in and out, they come and go. The fears, the frustrations — they must be borne, but not without hope.

Round and Round

Fightings and arguments, prosecutions and defenses, bickerings and quarrelings — I'm glad that isn't all that I remember. I can recall repentance and forgiveness, remorse and reconciliation. I guess we must learn the gospel the hard way, but the waste of it all, the stumbling blocks to the spread of the gospel! We could have done with less of it. The differences and disagreements must be, but when they are extended into hates and grudges, hardness and division, this is insufferable, a shame. When we fail in our fellowship, we belie the gospel we preach. Returning missionaries carry their peeves back with them and they get a chance for a new start over there, but the bitterness left in the hearts of the Japanese who sat at their feet goes on and on. Many scars remain in the body of Christ where the contrary missionary took his stand and turned his sword against his brothers. If it were not for the all-sufficient grace of Christ, the all-sufficient church would fracture itself to dust. Only when love for one another is learned can the multitude of sins be covered and the wounds healed.

On and On

I have seen the goodness of the Lord in the land of the living! I have seen the sun rise over the vineyard, and its golden rays dance among the lucious clusters of hanging grapes. I have reached forth and tasted the delicious fruit. Yes, as some go back and forth, in and out, up and down, there are those faithful Japanese Christians who go on and on. With their roots in the earth, and their hearts in heaven, they bring forth fruit, more fruit, and much fruit. In the midst of change and decay they remain steady, on course. The genuineness of their faith cannot be doubted. The word of Christ in their lives cannot be denied. The work in the Japan harvest field is slow, rugged and hard, but is there an easy field? Wherever the gospel seed is sown, in due season we shall reap, if we faint not. God's will is being done on earth when we continue steadfastly sowing and reaping. On and on we must go, and one day, when it is all over we shall meet in heaven a lot of brothers and sisters who used to speak Japanese, who used to live across the wide Pacific. And they will be there because we and they kept on and on in the service of our Lord and Master, Jesus Christ.

1. YOU SUCCEED WITHOUT SUCCESS

And all these, though well attested by their faith, did not receive what was promised. — HEBREWS 11:39

Being brought up in the tradition that success is the measure of a man, missionary work has proven to be full of frustrations that irritate, and irritations that frustrate. Things never seem to work out the way you want them, when you want them. I've tried being the highpowered executive type, but always end up doing everything myself. I've tried being the non-direct, all-knowing psychologist type, and ended up accomplishing nothing. Why can't natives, oops! I mean nationals, be more interested in my success as a missionary?

Again, we read in our religious papers about the great successes of missionaries in this or that country, and I find myself wishing I was there. How come the work is hard going only in the place where I am? Why are the nationals where I am not flocking to hear the gospel? Why do the people I love remain indifferent and cold? Maybe those papers do what I do and only print the good stuff. Maybe they aren't telling the whole truth. Is it possible that behind it all others are not roaring successes either? I try to cover up all my failures, and never tell my supporters about them, for fear I will become a "financial failure." Wouldn't it be just a bit comforting to read, "Preacher Returned from Overseas Admits Very Little Accomplished," or, "Baptized One Hundred Yesterday; Can't Find Ninety Today."

One thing I like about the Bible — it tells the whole story. If the lives of men of God recorded there were put into headlines you would read, "After a Lifetime of Hard Work and Suffering

Jeremiah Passes into Obscurity with Nothing to Show for It." Or about Christ before Pilate, "After Three Years' Work Not One Convert Remains Faithful."

Success isn't everything, but doing the will of the Lord is. Certainly there are successes in doing God's will, but they are not always obvious. Success in the sight of God could mean enduring failures in the sight of men. Overzealous advocates of Pauline methodology who promise success if Paul's "formula" is followed, need the headline which would read, "Paul Fails to Establish Church in Rome, the World's Most Strategic Center; Misses by Twenty Years; Methods Considered Unsuccessful."

The missionary preacher is not called to success, but to faithfulness. He is not sent to baptize, but to preach the gospel. The work is to be done to please Christ, not to please readers. He is not to be judged by *a* sponsoring church, but *the* sponsoring Christ! The fruit of success, or the promise of his labors may not be experienced in his lifetime. His faith may be the testimonial and not his success. In the chapter of Hebrews quoted above, along with the successes are listed the dismal failures, but the chief point is faith which surmounts difficulties, faith which endures faithfully, though that which was promised was not received. Some churches will only back a work fulfilled, but faithful churches will back a work unfulfilled. They will sow in hope, and endure until God's purposes are accomplished. Great will be their reward for they will have succeeded without success.

2. MISSIONARY WITH A CAPITAL "M"

For it is not the man who commends himself that is accepted, but the man whom the Lord commends.
— II Corinthians 10:18

I've been told that I don't look like a missionary, and I don't know whether that's good or bad, but I can remember one occasion when I thought it was good. Not knowing I was a missionary, a national said to me, as he pointed out a missionary passing by, "I hate missionaries, they think they own everything and act like big shots." Being a Cannon, I could not see anything wrong with a big shot, but nevertheless my friend was irritated and he irritated me. I think I know what he was driving at, though.

Most of us landed on the mission field just ordinary fellows, and from average to poor families at that. But all of a sudden we are now foreign dignitaries, ambassadors, rich capitalists. Wow! This is about all our poor humble heads can stand. We get looked at wherever we go; we are like movie stars; we are important; we are just discovering how wonderful we are! Surely the little native churches must recognize this, too. We can tell them how things should be run. Didn't I just meet the mayor? Don't I have more money than the average fellow here? (Generally more than the average mayor.) Why, it soon becomes known in most places that every one who becomes a Christian must first be baptized by the missionary. I know places where baptisms are stored up until the *Missionary* arrives — what a grand harvest! The capital "M" can take credit for the whole works and write a fine report. I can remember "fudging" on somebody else's labor myself. A few "borrowed baptisms" here and there can enhance one's stature.

Now the nature of foreign evangelistic work is such that big egos go starving for attention. Turning to the world, the capital "M" can find numerous outlets for self-commendation. He can find a "place in the sun." Instant praise can be found for all charitable endeavors and for all observable phenomena. The system is there. The Appointment, the Presentation, the Pictures, the Reporters, the Certificate, the Banquet of Honor. Good works should not be avoided, but most of the honors can be avoided with a little presence of mind. Anyway capital "M" can find "missionary work" very self-satisfying.

I was reprimanded by a fellow missionary once for trying to get native Christians to stop calling me capital "M", and he said "They will always exalt the missionary above everyone else, so just accept the title and let it go at that." Well, I have never taken to being bossed around religiously, or any other way, and I wondered if there might be some nationals who felt the same way. After a few discreet inquiries, lo and behold! I found out that most of them felt the same as I! They wanted us all to be brothers, as the Lord taught, and that in most cases capital "M" was exalted not because of love and respect, but because he held the purse strings, and cut a big figure.

Preachers, we do not need to capitalize on the opportunities to commend ourselves. The passage from II Corinthians, by the way, which is the greatest defense of missionary work ever written, teaches us to wait for the Lord's commendation. When it comes, it will be genuine, not built upon false titles and positions, but upon truth. Not according to "other men's labors," nor "another's field," but according to what we really are, and what we really have done.

3. HOMING PIGEONS

And John left them and returned to Jerusalem
— ACTS 13:13

A barber in Oklahoma told me about his homing pigeons he used in racing. It seems they take these birds hundreds of miles away, and then release them, and no matter where they are released they race on a beeline straight for home. Not knowing much about these birds, I was amazed at such infallible instincts and sense of direction. Later I was to observe a similar phenomena on the mission field. It seemed that no matter where a missionary was sent, it would be no time at all until he was home again, safe and sound!

Recently, I saw some statistics that listed missionaries sent out over the past twenty years. The figures showed twice as many now residing at home as there were on the field! Not knowing a missionary yet that didn't leave the field for good reasons, I have always considered the reasons he came to the field far superior. I'm sure John Mark gave a good reason for returning to Jerusalem, but it didn't help those who were left behind. Tragedies have terminated a missionary's work against his own will, but I'm persuaded that this is not so in many cases.

Why is the casualty rate so high? The list of reasons is long, but the reasons voiced and the actual cause can be two different things. I have always admired the candor of the missionary who gave the real reason for leaving: "I hate these people and can't stand them any longer." This is better than some of the lame excuses like, "I've done my share," or "I'm needed back in the States." Needs always exist there, but there are greater needs where Christ is unknown. Also, *what* is our share? The average life of a missionary on a field is about two years they say. The shares of those who remain on the field increase with the time, as they have to pick up the pieces left by the short-timer. Those who have "served their time" talk like missionary work is a stretch in the penitentiary, after which they are free to go home. Perhaps they feel like they came to the field as birds in cages, trapped by bars of time and circumstance. Now they can fly home.

I realize that anyone who stays on the field, does so, not by his own goodness, but by the grace of Christ. And this is the heart of the matter. Heart trouble! When you take the mission out of the missionary he must pack up and leave. Somewhere along the line the canary has forgotten his song. The grace of Christ is forgotten, the joy that comes from dedicated service no longer is present. Other matters have crowded in, and the mission has been crowded out, and the heart is troubled.

We can be encouraged though; John Mark did not give up forever. We find him reactivated and once more serving with Barnabas, with Paul, and others. The good work begun must be continued. The grace that brought us out of ourselves and into foreign fields can do it again. But our hearts must be willing; we must find our home wherever the grace of Christ leads us, and some day we will be released from the prison of humiliation and fly home to be with our Lord above.

4. A MISSIONARY AND HIS MONEY ARE SOON PARTED

He scatters abroad, he gives to the poor.
— II Corinthians 9:9

"Have mercy on me thou son of David and buy me a motorcycle," read the words on a note handed to me at the front door. I may be soft in the head, but I'm not that soft. I gave him a cup of tea instead. He asked me for something I couldn't give him, but he received what I could give him. All requests are not like this one, but enough of them are that you have to be discerning.

I have met very few missionaries that were not as generous as the day is long. We know that too much money can be a handicap, but I have never met a missionary with too much money. It is true that he walks into the country flush and eager, but he doesn't stay that way long. He is met with wretched poverty and crying needs. He is appalled at the ignorance of the people concerning the gospel of Christ. He sees so many ways in which to work and do good that he soon finds himself over-extended. I hear there are some who oppose the subsidization of native work on the grounds that it would spoil the natives. Well, that would depend on how the money is administered and what the people are like. I would rather risk over-extension, than under-extension. A miser is not going to lead people to Christ. What about wasting money? There isn't a Christian in the world that hasn't done some of that, and we missionaries share in their guilt. But I have seen a little go a long way in the hands of a generous missionary. Sometimes what we may consider wastefulness, can really be generosity. If I understand the Scriptures correctly, God is generous and scatters blessings everywhere. Are we to be less than this? If God gives to the poor, is not this money down a rat hole? Don't we have the poor with us always? But God makes a poor investment in those from which He gets no return because he loves and sympathizes.

It happens also that while the missionary is committing his funds more and more, his supporters commit them less and less. If a missionary goes out to a field for five years, no one raises his salary for five years, regardless of the circumstances. I know a missionary who didn't get a raise for seven years. Not only that, but he had to face the unpleasant experience of "Dear John" letters that say, "Because we are reorganizing our budget for the next fiscal year and concentrating our funds on a different work, we wish to inform you that beginning next month our contribution to your work will be terminated." Oh, brother! As the demands of your work increase the support of it decreases. Do you think that this is an exception? I could wear out your ears with concrete examples. I know a missionary who was "forgotten" for six months. Fortunately his Boss in Heaven didn't forget, so he kept eating.

Out of sight — out of mind! How true this saying is! Maybe this is one reason men do not stay in foreign fields very long, but honor to those sterling characters who put up with the shabby treatment and thoughtlessness of their supporters to work the will of God. A missionary and his money may soon be parted, but let's not hurry the process along with our own inconsideration.

5. ARE YOU ESTABLISHING INDIGENOUS CHURCHES?

Rather speaking the truth in love, we are to grow up in every way into him, who is the head, into Christ, from whom the whole body joined and knit together by every joint with which it is applied, when each part is working properly, makes bodily growth and upbuilds itself in love. — EPHESIANS 4:15-16

The expert looked me in the eye and said, "What do you suggest we do to reach the missionary's goal of establishing indigenous churches?" I didn't mean to be rude, but I answered, "That's not this missionary's goal." My friend stiffened a little at this for he was of the persuasion that "the responsibility of the missionary on the field is to build self-governing, self-propagating, and self-supporting native churches." I don't want to be contrary, but I have always thought of my goal and responsibility as a missionary in a different light. With Paul, I feel like my responsibility is "to preach the gospel" and establish Christ-minded, Christ-loving, Christ-supporting Christians. After all, you can have self-governing, etc. churches that are selfish, not willing to love and help others. It is possible to have a church of self-propagating devils. You can have self-supporting, sectarian, and anti-every-good-work churches. So obviously there is more involved here than the surface accruements of independent church government. Establishing an independent native Christianity can be as repulsive as that of native nationalism. In fact, in the New Testament, we find many things to the contrary. Brethren are taught to enlarge their hearts and be a part of interdependent Christianity rather than independent Christianity.

I tried this approach on a "native" church once, sounding very wise as I said, "You need to develop native Japanese Christianity." They had me know right away that they were interested in the New Testament kind of Christianity, and that to exist as Christians they had to fight many objectionable elements of Japanese society. Needless to say, I changed the subject.

Being an heir to the Restoration Movement, I must ask the question, "Do these terms represent Scriptural ideas?" "Does the gospel seed sown in many lands produce the kind of churches described by these terms?" For a number of years I had considered the churches I worked with indigenous because, well, that was the thing to do. Finally, I decided to look up the word (I know, my ignorance is showing) and now I'm not so sure I'd like to establish indigenous churches. In fact, I'm not so sure I can. Indigenous means "Originating in a specified place or country." Christianity originated in Palestine where the "Word of the Lord went out from Jerusalem" (Isaiah 2:2), for "Salvation is of the Jews" (John 4:22). I'm not so sure it "originated" there, because it came with Christ from Heaven. If I understand the Scriptures and history correctly, Christianity was brought into this world, and from Jerusalem was carried into all the countries of the world. As a missionary, I carry the seed into a country, but God, not a group of nationals, begets it.

In the New Testament the whole church is described as one united body, with every one depending on the other, and local churches depending on each other, as per the text of this section. Independence can mean isolation, and isolation death. Interdependence can mean "bodily growth . . . up-building itself in love."

6. LOOK OUT, HERE COMES THE NEW MISSIONARY!

Let no one despise your youth, but set the believers an example in speech and conduct, in love, in faith, in purity. — I TIMOTHY 4:12

18

I don't despise my younger fellow-missionaries, but I've sure learned to duck. They come hot, zealous, and gunnin' for game. They are ready to shoot at anything that moves, and I've got the scars to prove it. Everything is different to them, and therefore something must be wrong. They are ready to reform the whole works, purge out the old leaven, and revolutionize all procedures. The trouble in dealing with them is the fact that sometimes they are right. There's nothing like new blood to get things stirring, but who wants ulcers stirred up. I am sure criticism has its place, but brother, could you smile a little when you level it?

Whenever I hear of a new missionary coming, I feel like running to the hills. What will he oppose? How many native brethren will he offend? Will he be an anti? How shall we meet the threat and the challenge? Of course, sometimes the fears are for nothing and the man turns out to be fairly reasonable. Over a period of time, things work out all right, but the period of adjustment and needed experience can be a hectic one.

Yet, I have never met better men. They have to be independent; they have to be tough to get to the field in the first place. Older missionaries had to put up with a lot from me in my day. A lot of the good advice was wasted on me. How hard it is for a young man to be wise. I guess most of us have to learn the hard way. Good mission work takes close cooperation, but new workers want to go it alone, and you pray that they will last long enough to realize it. It seems everybody wants to be Paul and nobody wants to be Timothy. At least our married men should be willing to settle for being a Peter! Anyway, new missionary, hang loose and learn!

I've been caught in the middle of a dilemma; if I dished out advice I was accused of being too bossy; if I didn't say anything they were being ignored and didn't know what was going on! Patience, let us all learn patience, and let it have its perfect work. We must learn to work together, and the grace of Christ makes it possible. There are too many battles to fight shoulder to shoulder to be drawing on one another. Let no one despise your youth, but also remember there are good reasons for grey hair — find them out!

7. MISSIONARY ACCIDENTS AND GOD'S PROVIDENCE

> *And they went through the region of Phrygia and Galatia, having been forbidden by the Holy Spirit to speak the word in Asia. And when they had come opposite Mysia, they attempted to go into Bithynia, but the Spirit of Jesus did not allow them.*
>
> — ACTS 16:6-7

You know, it's a wonder that anything is accomplished for the Lord. The only times I have felt really wise were the occasions when the Lord did something I subsequently claimed to have done. In this is a sin, one we are too prone to — accepting glory for ourselves when we know good and well that it belongs to our Lord. "For apart from me you can do nothing" are words of truth of which we need to be reminded. There have been times when I have begged for the grace of Christ to make a way for me, and when it was made I acted like I did it myself. Have you ever done a benevolent work out of the love of Christ in you, and then after it was recognized, and you were praised, you took the reward like you deserved it? How easy it is for a pure motivation to be polluted.

Yes! Plans need to be made, and God-given talents used, but we had better keep our ears tuned to God's providence. Paul and his company had their own ideas as to where they should go, and when they should go, but the Lord disagreed with them. Being men of God, they accepted guidance of the Spirit and finally went where God wanted them to go. How perplexed they must have been.

I have had finely-laid plans fall to pieces, and though I complained at the time, I have found that God had better plans in mind. I have found more than once, that an accidental straying from a certain plan accomplished even more than what we had in mind! I have been made to look wise when the work is done, but I remember my wisdom was foolishness, and I thank God that I didn't get my own way. It is sometimes an excruciating experience, but I am learning a little of what it is like to work with God. We are filled so much with our own importance, that we don't leave any elbow room for Christ. He is with us,

"Yea, even unto the end of the world," but do we leave any room for His suggestions? After all, He is head of the church, not us. His will is to be done, not ours. If Paul had some set methods about his work, they didn't always please the Lord. According to the text we can consider them on this occasion "forbidden," and "not allowed." Our ideas are not going to fare any better if we want to do the will of Christ. I don't know about you, but I am often apt to take my completed plans to Christ for His approval, rather than consulting Him before they are made. This makes for a lot of back-tracking, and "loss of face." The purpose of the missionary is not to show how wise and successful he is, but to show the grace of Christ working in his weaknesses to the glory of the Lord. This is a hard nut to swallow, but it is actually the case. We tend to give a different impression though. We want to think that the grace of Christ is shown in our strength so we can have something to boast about. But you can see that this is inconsistent and impossible. Grace is shown to be grace in weaknesses, not in strengths. So in admitting and recognizing our weaknesses it becomes possible for Christ's will to be done. God's plans can now be carried out in our work, and God's name will be glorified. I fear that many of the methods, and many of the fancy names given to them by the brotherhood, glorify man's wisdom and not God's.

Let us watch now for the seeming accidents, for the interruptions of our thinking and planning. It may be God trying to open up for us a way of acceptable, rewarding service for Him.

8. HARVEST FIELDS?

For here the saying holds true, "One sows and another reaps." I sent you to reap that for which you did not labor; others have labored, and you have entered into their labor. — JOHN 4:37-38

It seems that the whole church is in favor of going to the harvest fields. Our young men and women are challenged to go out and reap the harvest. We say, "The whole world is ripe unto harvest!" Well, I'm sorry to say, this is not true. What a shocking experience it is for missionaries to go out under the impression that they are going to a harvest field and find out that it is just a field! Sometimes a rocky, weedy one at that! They find that the people of that country are not "ripe unto harvest." They are faced with the prospect of a life of hard unrewarding labor. They are unprepared for this. There they are with a scythe in their hand when it ought to be a plough, a basket for the fruits instead of a bag of seed. It's enough to disillusion many a young person, and many a young person it does.

The world is the field, but it is not just a harvest field. It is a land for sowing, and watering, and waiting and gathering. Everyone is eager for the dramatic, rewarding experience of harvesting, but not the same for the ploughing and sowing. Even some who are considered experts in missionary work advocate putting all of our resources into those areas and countries where we are getting a harvest. Certainly we must reap, but it is contrary to the Great Commission of Christ to reap only. "Go ye into *all* the world and preach. . . ." Sowing *always* precedes the harvest. We are looking for something for nothing when we are willing only to reap. We are looking for the cream without milking the cow!

Now, if you happen to be reaping, let the Lord remind you that "you reap that for which you did not labor." Harvesting involves work all right, but it was preceded by hard labor. Those who pride themselves in the number of baptisms they administer, or the results of their great meetings, need to bow the knee and thank God for those who sowed. They had better not claim the harvest for themselves, but rather so work "that sower and reaper may rejoice together."

It's a poor commentary on our Christianity when we are not willing to pay the price that it takes to sow. Some churches have actually switched from a work that was a sowing proposition to one that was a reaping one. Desertion on the field of battle it is called, an action of cowards and self-seekers. They are working for themselves, not for God. They would rather "switch than fight." They walk the path of least resistance. They will not be able to rejoice together with the sower.

Missionary work must be done with great patience and endurance. We "sow in hope" in many places around the world. It takes preparation and dedication to do this, and many prayers by Christians back home. You may not be able to immediately justify the time and expense with a glowing report. Some missionaries are not satisfied that anything is being done unless there are baptisms! Let us not be so shallow and lacking in spiritual insight as to require a harvest before the time. Be satisfied when you are patiently sowing the word, and send young men and women who are willing to do this, who are willing to wait until, when in God's good providence, harvest time comes. It may not come for a hundred years, but come it will and there will be rejoicing in heaven as well as on earth.

Missionary friends, let us stop frustrating ourselves by continually requiring a harvest. Supporting Christians, stop being impatient with your sowers. Churches, as your eyes are caught by the "fields white unto harvest," remember the sowers. As you send forth reapers, remember "others have labored, and you have entered into their labor." Christ reminded the disciples that they were not the pioneers among the Samaritans, others had labored before them. Prophets had watered the seed with their own blood. The disciples were but partners with those who had gone before. Let us not act like the harvest is the result of our own great power. God gave the increase to that which was sown by faithful planters of His in days gone by.

9. TOURING SERVICE — WE NEVER CLOSE

Jesus left the temple and was going away, when his disciples came to point out to him the buildings of the temple. — MATTHEW 24:1

One of his disciples said to him, 'Look Teacher, what wonderful stones and what wonderful buildings!' And Jesus said to him, 'Do you see these great buildings? There will not be left here one stone upon another, that will not be thrown down.
— MARK 13:1-2

Somehow I get the impression that Jesus didn't care an awful lot about a tour of the temple. What He said certainly squelched the enthusiasm of His disciples concerning the value of such an excursion. It caused me to think twice about the many tours our brethren are taking here and there. It's possible that they are a waste of time and of little interest to their Lord. The Lord implies that there is not much lasting value in viewing wonderful stones and great buildings that will soon be thrown down and destroyed. We are told that even beautiful scenery is stored up for fire. I don't want to be a killjoy, but the earth and its works is just a big pile of kindling wood as far as Christ is concerned.

Some tours are justified on "religious grounds": "See the missionary work," "See the Holy Land!" But I'm afraid that this may not be the true motivation. I was trying to get some elders to tour our work on purely "religious grounds," and one of them said to me, "Joe, I've seen the work by faith; I'd rather send you the money it would cost that the work might be helped." Scratch one great tour!

Someone told me the other day of an experienced preacher who couldn't get the travel funds he needed to go to a mission field, and I thought of all the money some Christians spend on pleasure trips, and sight-seeing. Careful there now! I don't oppose reasonable recreation, but I oppose all pleasure that is enjoyed at the expense of the work of the church and our spiritual development. We need to justify our pleasure on religious grounds.

Even the religious tours have their drawbacks. I feel the need for having elders and supporters in the States who have seen the work, but I wonder how much they really understand? They come green as gourds and take a surface view of what is going on. Some have landed in a country where it is harvest time, and have exclaimed, "Look at all the good they are doing." Whereas in another place, where the going is tough, and there isn't much showing yet, "There's not much going on here." Thus, some work suffers from surface comparison. Knowing this tendency to judge by outward appearance it was a relief to me to get a new building where I work, even though we are not working any harder than we did when we had the old, falling-down one. Our work makes a better impression now!

How many hours and how many dollars have missionaries

spent on touring Christians from home churches? Like other people we enjoy having visitors from time to time, but I know a missionary who quit the field because visitors imposed so much on his time and money! If you are on a pleasure trip you should make this clear, and leave the missionary free to do whatever he wants to about it.

If you are interested in the work, then it would be thoughtful to reimburse the missionary, and upon your return home get to work on his behalf, and in behalf of the cause of Christ there. Tours to places where you are supporting the work can be inspiring and helpful, and so can be the faith that works unceasingly for that which is unseen but eternal.

Well, after this, I guess no one will come to see me any more. You are really welcome you know, but let's make it a meaningful experience in Christ our Lord.

10. BEGGAR AND BENEFACTOR

We are fools for Christ's sake, but you are wise in Christ. We are weak, but you are strong. You are held in honor, but we in disrepute.
— I CORINTHIANS 4:10

He left the field saying, "From now on I'm going to become financially independent; I'm not going to be a beggar any more," and with this another fine man joined the ever burgeoning ranks of ex-missionaries.

Now whether you are a beggar or not depends upon your attitude, but nevertheless, if you are a missionary you are a beggar. It's a foregone conclusion. It's in the woof and warp of things. The only thing not settled is what kind of beggar you are going to be. I doubt if my friend will find the financial independence he has in mind, but he is free from the revolting system that treats men of God as beggars, and enhances contributors as benefactors.

We act like a contribution to a missionary work is the bestowal of a great favor on someone, instead of what it really is, an infinitesimal payment on a debt of love we owe to God, "to

Greek and barbarians, both to wise and unwise" (Romans 1: 14). Though I'm in the place of a beggar, I don't feel like one. That's the difference, I think, between that ex-missionary and the present missionary. The fact that Christ made Himself take on the form of the lowest beggar, encourages me to be the kind I am.

Now, I think most church members do not really mean to treat their overseas representatives in that way, but I get the distinct impression that they do it anyway. In some cases, instead of paying the missionary an adequate salary, he is placed in a position where the benefactors can feel sorry for him, and take up a special collection. He can be expected to get along on less than the average member, yet work harder than they do. When he comes around asking (shall we say begging?) for help in work we ought to be helping, we must determine whether or not we will bless him, as if it is to be for his own bread and butter. And beggar, another thing, don't forget your manners. Don't forget to say pretty please, and send thank-you notes, and written praise for the favor (wages) bestowed (paid) for what was given as a gift (owed) to Christ. The parentheses keep me from being beggarly in a disagreeable sense. Yet gladly do we beg for Christ's sake, but it does no honor for those who stand in the benefactors' shoes instead of in the shoes of a partner.

The first thing a new missionary must learn is that churches are not prepared to do what they are supposed to do, so he must hit the road to raise his own salary, raise his own travel fund, and raise his own hackles. This separates the he-men from the boys — fast! The high pressure salesman type gets the job done lickety-split, but what about the innocent, modest young man, who works well for the Lord, but not well for himself. Too bad, but he is going to be low man on the totem pole! He'll never get a raise until somebody feels sorry for him. Crippling debts will tax his energy, and he will be ripe for entering the ranks of the exes. There is something wrong in it all, and considerate supporters are seeing the light.

I have talked to many missionaries about this problem, and I thank God for the dedicated, uncomplaining guy that is getting the job done in spite of the benefactors' shortcomings. Let us not look at the work of the Lord as something we bestow our favors upon, whether beggar or benefactor, but rather let us be partners in repaying in some way a part of the great price that was paid for our salvation. And lets do it in such a way as will bring glory to Christ, and honor to the churches of Christ.

11. MISSIONARY METHODS – PAUL'S OR MINE?

I have become all things to all men, that I might by all means save some. – I CORINTHIANS 9:22

"You're not working like the Apostle Paul. Why don't you use the Pauline methods?" said my missionary friend, and for lack of a better answer, I said, "Because I married Rosa Belle and not Pauline (my wife's sister), and I'm not a methodist." It seems though that every time we get to talking about Paul's methods, I get steered to a fellow called Roland Allen and advised to read his book *Missionary Methods – St. Paul's or Ours?* Well, I found out Paul didn't write Roland Allen's book, so if you don't mind, I'd rather get it from the horse's mouth. In reading Acts, and the letters of Paul, for the life of me, Paul is not as dogmatic as Mr. Allen, and Paul doesn't seem to make any method clear at all. To the contrary, he sounds like he is willing to use any and/or all methods to lead souls to Christ.

I have met a few men who thought they were Apostle Pauls, but I never met a Christian yet that could fill his boots. He was one man that Christ chose to show "all His longsuffering through." None of us are that weak. We are all better than the "chief of sinners." He was chosen not to show what a great, successful, strong man he was, but rather how great the grace of Christ was in accomplishing such a great deal through such a weak vessel. I can be encouraged to follow the grace of Christ in a weak man like Paul, but I am mightily discouraged if I have to measure up to a strong, perfect Paul. Following a strong man like the Paul I read about in some missionary books would wear me out, but I have a chance with the Paul of the New Testament. He is not as picky about methods as some of our missionary methodologists, and he relies always on the grace of

Christ to get him out of the scrapes he gets in, and he attributes everything that he is to the grace of God. That means that Christ can make a gospel preacher out of me, too. It means that He can bless *my methods* and bring something good out of them. It means that even the weakest methods might be really the only ones that Christ will use to manifest His wonderful patience. You see, the methodologists are missing the boat here — they are after a formula that will guarantee missionary success, but there is no such thing! (They seem to want a strong method of operation but won't use it.) Paul's life shows what can be done with a weak, sinful vessel when it is filled with the grace of Christ! This is *the method* that Christ uses, and it brings good news to our ears. It means that in spite of our stupidity, or great intelligence (take your choice), Christ can use us to accomplish His mission in all the countries of the world. I'm not trying to justify failure or ignorance, but I am saying that real success as a missionary depends more on the grace of Christ than all the methods we use. I am also recognizing that I am not using all the methods Paul used, and that Paul did not use all the methods I use, but that Paul's mission and mine are the same; namely that by the *grace* of Christ we might "by *all methods* save some."

12. ARE YOU QUALIFIED TO BE A MISSIONARY?

Where did this man get this wisdom and these mighty works? Is not this the carpenter's son? Is not his mother called Mary? And are not his brothers James and Joseph and Simon and Judas? And are not all his sisters with us? Where then did this man get all this? And they took offense at him.
— MATTHEW 13:54-57

As you can see from the above, there was more than one way of looking at the qualifications of Jesus of Nazareth as the Christ, the Missionary Son of God, sent from Heaven to be the Saviour of Israel and the world. Likewise, there is more than one way of looking at the qualifications of one who walks in the steps of the Greatest Missionary (that's right, even greater than Paul) in the world.

I once read in a missionary magazine a list of all the things necessary to being a good missionary. Well, after that treatment I was ready to pack up and go home. I was obviously not qualified. The list of qualifications described a superman and super-Christians. But just as I was ready to call a travel agency I began to mull it over, and I thought, "I have met a lot of missionaries. Have I ever met one that had all of those qualifications? No, I haven't! Well, then, how did all of these fellows get into missionary work?" I felt better after that. But then, later someone hit me with the Apostle Paul, and how qualified he was to do missionary work, and that did it. I certainly was not like Paul, and my work couldn't hold a candle to his, so I thought I might better serve the Lord by getting out of His way on the missionfield. My in-laws wanted their daughter back, and my mother didn't want me to go in the first place. I remembered also that while I was in college Teacher A thought I wasn't good enough to do successful missionary work, and Teacher B thought I was too good to go to the missionary field. I guess Teacher A was right after all. Then I got mad. I wasn't sent to the mission field by Teacher A, or B, nor by Paul, nor by that missionary magazine. Jesus Christ sent me. It was His idea. He's my boss, and I love Him, and when I saw the hard time people gave Him because they thought He wasn't qualified to be their Saviour, I concluded that Jesus and I were in the same boat, so why worry about the thunder and the storm.

You know, there's more to this qualification business than meets the eye. I'm for better training of men and women we send out into the world to preach the gospel, and our Christian schools need to "get on the ball" about it, but at the same time, this matter of who is qualified to go isn't determined by us. Although some churches may not now have Mission Boards and Examining Committees that determine who the churches should send to the mission field, don't think they aren't on the horizon! Somebody is going to come up with a test or a computer conclusion as to who should, and who should not go. Well, I'm not like Paul in everything, but I'm with him on "not conferring with flesh and blood (Galatians 1:16) about a God-given mission. When Christ says "Come, follow me, and I will make you fishers of men" (Matthew 4:19) you shouldn't say, "Wait, Lord, until I consult with my superiors about it." Men with a mission get to the mission field, and in most cases I know, in spite of opposition from the people.

And I want to say something about those who have all the degrees needed to qualify for missionary work. I haven't seen them hanging around on the mission field any longer than anybody else. I'm not saying that training wouldn't help you to do a better job. It should help you. But what I am saying is this: a man is a missionary whom the Lord qualifies, not men. This is the freedom God's man has, and it is justified by what he does, and not by what people think of him. Jesus was Messiah and Saviour in fact, proven by what He did, even though He was disqualified in the minds of leaders, teachers, and hometown folks. Here let us take courage and move on.

13. PATERNALISM

For though you have ten thousand tutors in Christ, yet have you not many fathers; for in Christ Jesus I begat you through the gospel. — I CORINTHIANS 4:15

There is a unique and special relationship that exists between the missionary preacher and the native converts. Call it whatever you want to, it is still there and will always be there. It is not just an emotional thing, but involves the reality of time and effort, of concern and love as the evangelist works for the salvation of souls. This sacred relationship should not be taken lightly by the missionary. It is not just a matter of running in, preaching the gospel, and running out again. This kind of action does not recognize the responsibility of caring for precious souls that are born anew under one's teaching. It can be called "child desertion." I am convinced in my own mind that the apostle Paul was not guilty of this kind of thing, even though I get the distinct impression from some that he hurried from place to place, not spending much time anywhere, and completing each job as he went. Paul never retired from a fatherly relationship he held with those who were converted under his preaching. As per the above verse, though there were many others who came after him to teach the converts, he always cared about them, and was always concerned about them (II Corinthians 11:28). If the churches established by Paul were always self-sufficient, why would he need to return to visit them? Why write letters of command and exhortation? The nature of churches and things is such as demands the continuance of a love relationship.

Now, missionaries who go to foreign fields, start a work, and then leave it forever, are "child deserters." They can be accused of promiscuous irresponsibility. Many have been the times that children begotten by certain missionaries have asked me, "Whatever happened to brother so and so?" "Is he coming back to us?" "Why doesn't he write?" Many have been the trials of good men who have been persuaded by missionaries to quit good jobs to work full time with them in the gospel, only to have their support abruptly terminated, or to be "forgotten" by sponsoring churches, or "dumped" in the name of self-support, or "deserted" by the "Vanishing American." Many have been the startings and stoppings of churches vigorously commenced only to be thoroughly dropped. What shall we say about this? I know there is such a thing as being over-paternalistic, stifling the initiative of nationals and their churches. It is not true fatherhood to do everything always for children. But I would like to say this. What is needed most of all on the mission field is more of the right kind of paternalism. More fatherly feeling, more concern for native Christians, more fatherly direction.

Some churches don't want to "subsidize foreign mission work." They don't want to "spoil" the natives. I'll tell them the quickest and surest way of spoiling the natives, and that is to withhold food when the children are crying for it, withhold shelter when the storms are beating around, and then desert them before they can even walk! There is a time when the children mature and must strike out on their own, but don't leave them before that time! Don't try to unnaturally hurry their growth so that you can boast of a successful, self-supporting work. Before leaving them to make their own way, make sure that you have been a father to them, and that you will never forsake that relationship though continents and seas should separate you. New missionary! Prospective missionary! Are you willing and able to take on the responsibility of fatherhood? I hope so. Think about it. Pray about it!

14. THE MISSIONARY MIND OF CHRIST AND THE AMERICAN MIND OF THE MISSIONARY

Have this mind in you, which was also in Christ Jesus. — PHILIPPIANS 2:5

I have never met a missionary who would admit that he was teaching Americanism instead of Christianity. I always told the native brethren, "I'm teaching you nothing except New Testament Christianity." There is nothing wrong with holding this worthy goal in mind, but I am not so sure that I have always done this. After all, we have been brought up in a materialistic, money-oriented society and it takes a great struggle to shift gears to "setting our minds on things above" (Colossians 3:2).

When a missionary lands in a foreign country, his mind immediately begins to make comparisons with things back home. While new ideas and customs challenge him, well, "There's no place like home." Everything suffers from a comparison with the "American Way of Life," the "Greatest Country in the World," etc. The net result can easily be a quick trip home, and, or an insufferable, arrogant state of mind.

Now, the thing for each missionary, yea, for each Christian, to do is to learn the mind of Christ — to think as the Greatest Missionary thought, and to live in a foreign country as He lived in this foreign world. When this is done, we find our American minds in basic conflict with the mind of Christ. Let us look at some instances where this could be true.

The Scripture quoted above goes on to tell us what the mind of Christ is like (Philippians 2:5-8). He was "equal with God." He didn't have to stir up a revolution in order to make a power-grab. In other words, He "had it made." He had everything.

He was the equal of a "billionaire." Yet He changed all this. He left it behind and "emptied himself." All the profit became loss. I guess it would be equivalent to a kind of voluntary bankruptcy contrary to good enterprising business principles. He turned success into failure. Can our American minds understand this? Not only that, He took on "the form of a slave." He gave up what we Americans revere and strive after all our days: freedom and independence! To think of becoming a slave is detestable, yet this was the mind of Christ! Does this justify slavery? I don't know much about politics and things like that, but I do know that it justifies slaving among men for the sake of God. Again, He was "made in the likeness of men!" Can you imagine it? He became earthy. He took His abode in a house of mud. He took unsanitary conditions unto Himself. This doesn't mean that He didn't bathe, but it means that He would need to bathe continually. With the American mind so fussy about germs, sanitation, sterilization and cleanliness, it would be hard to subject oneself to these conditions. Am I justifying unsanitary practices? Of course not, but if you are going to have the missionary mind of Christ, you will have to learn to put up with them in order to do God's will. Again, He was "found in fashion as a man," says the Scriptures. Borrowing Madison Avenue for a minute, we find that He "projected" a poor "image." He did not maintain good status. A superman image would have met the requirements of human minds, but rather than the fashion of an angel, He lived like a man, and projected an image capable of being misunderstood. And misunderstood it was. It was so repulsive it was unacceptable to high society, and worse than that, was nailed to a cross. Not only did He give the appearance of an ordinary slave, He went and "humbled Himself" even further. Instead of promoting Himself, advertising Himself, He made Himself of no reputation. A nobody! He didn't maintain a public-pleasing name. Then we have the last straw! He became "obedient even unto death, yea, the death of the cross." He didn't take good care of Himself. To obey death is contrary to the "pursuit of happiness." He sacrificed health, ambition, everything to die on a cross. This type of religious fanaticism just won't go in America. We want success! He chose what the world calls failure!

Now, the missionary mind of Christ, by doing this, showed us that He was not living for Himself, but for God. He was not seeking His own profit, but the profit of others. He was not seeking happiness for Himself alone, but for others. He was not advertising Himself, but Another. He was not interested in His own image, but in the Image of God. This is the missionary mind of Christ, and how contrary it is so many times to the American mind of us missionaries!

15. THE MISSIONARY'S GREATEST PROBLEM

And there arose a sharp contention, so that they separated from each other. — ACTS 15:39

It seems that one of the reasons that sent David Livingstone north into unexplored jungle was his disgust at the disputes between "missionaries north of the river and those south of it." Do you know of a mission field where the missionaries have not fought and divided, or are not at present fighting and dividing? All it seems to take is a little difference of some kind, and it becomes a big difference. A little difference in geography, a little difference in methods of work, a little difference in the Christian college you graduated from and BOOM! Big, big, big differences. Certainly, like marriage, there are differences that have to be worked out, and some disputes cannot be avoided, but why all the divorce? Divorce is to be avoided and differences solved because of the greater unity of love. "The unity of the Spirit in the bond of Peace" is more important than any of the quarrels, differences, and divisions among missionaries that I have ever heard about or experienced. I can remember there was a time in Ibaraki, Japan, when it seemed that the only thing we missionaries could agree on was baseball and food. If someone sponsored a social gathering, we would all meet and eat. If a ball game was coming up, we would be there to play. Kind of strange, don't you think? I hate to think that the only thing that kept us from dividing was a sandwich and a baseball! The Kuji River was a kind of rough dividing line in those days separating "my work" and "your work." Later the Tone River came in between the Ibaraki work and the Tokyo work! I am glad those days are in the past, and I hope the missionaries now have more sense, and more love than we had.

Aside from what division does to "your work," and "my work," what does it do to the Lord's work? What is the effect of preaching the unity of New Testament Christianity, and demonstrating the division of twentieth-century Christianity? To say the least, it disillusions the native brethren, and sets a bad example. Have you ever been asked, "Why do you missionaries hate one another?" "Why won't you associate with one another?" I used to answer, "Well, you Japanese have your fusses too." It wasn't much of an answer I'll admit. We are the ones obligated to demonstrate actions commensurate with unity in Christ. Problems cannot be avoided, but they can be dealt with. Having a problem in a mission field is not a shame. Satan is working to disrupt us all the time. But failing to solve it in brotherly love and understanding *is* a shame! Our native brethren cannot avoid disputes either, but they should be shown how to settle them amicably. Even the great men of the New Testament church had "sharp contention," but they reconciled their differences.

The greatest problem that a missionary will have, will be with another missionary. The problem is really within the individual missionary himself though. Among missionaries there are not "good guys" and "bad guys" (they're not all angels either), but they are men of God who need to love more and be loved more. They need to realize that "middle walls of partition" are "broken down," by the longsuffering of a cross (Ephesians 2: 13-16). We must be willing to sacrifice ourselves to one another, as Christ sacrificed Himself for us, in order to have the unity with one another that Christ has with us. This patience of the cross is hard to find in young, eager missionaries, but without it, their fondest dreams of their work for the Lord will never be fulfilled. You, missionary, are your greatest problem! What are you going to do about it?

16. GOING HOME FOR A REST OR ARE YOU KIDDING?

And he said to them, "Come away by yourselves to a lonely place and rest a while" . . . and they went away in the boat to a lonely place by themselves. Now many saw them going, and knew them, and they ran there on foot from all the towns, and got there ahead of them. — MARK 6:31-33

My preacher friend said, "It's nice that you are going to your home country for a rest, isn't it?" Innocently I replied, as I felt the bones pushing against my skin, "Yes, I'm looking forward to it." Little did I realize what was in store for us. Hot roast beef was steaming in my mind, and bass were jumping from one side of my head to the other. I could hardly wait!

Well, here we are, home at last! Trot out my slippers and an easy chair, I'm on furlough now! What's that? There are thirty churches who will cut off my support if I don't get around and speak to them? OK, but I'll be right back. Off we go, back we come. "Joe, the church here wants you to visit the following twenty members." All right, off we go. Back we come. Where's that easy chair? What, something else? Oh, I see you mean we can't expect people to put us up indefinitely? Well, I don't want to impose on anyone. I need to study somewhere anyway. It takes money to study. Money? I had forgotten about that! How are we going to finance this furlough? The churches know we are home, now, so they don't have to contribute to our work anymore. "Let us know when you are ready to go back," they say, "and we will send you some money." Thanks a lot. Well, it looks like I'll have to work during this rest period. What can I do? Nobody wants me for a few months only. If I haven't been preaching long, nobody wants me anyway.

"Hello, Joe," my jolly preacher friend says to me, "You missionaries are really lucky getting all this time off! And travel expenses paid at that!" I grimaced, and hated to tell him that we had borrowed the money we came home on. We would have to stay a long time in order to repay the loan and refinance our return journey. It would be easier not to go back.

I think I could really get some bass if I settled down and forgot about missionary work!

Oops! I forgot to mention the relatives! They have a few things to say you know! "No visible means of support, eh Joe?" "When are you going to get a job?" "Why did you go over there in the first place?" If you go and visit them, don't stay too long. Get a motel, and pay for it out of the unsteady income you have. "Oh, their poor kids. They drag them from pillar to post."

I got a job once, and the essence went like this, "Eleven years on the mission field, huh? Well, you'll still have to start at the bottom." Here we are treated like we just got out of school. Like we were just starting all over again! It must be because we look so young! That's a nice thought, but you can't hide all those kids! Another preacher friend again, "How are you enjoying your rest, Joe old boy? You lucky dog you!" The dog part, I agreed with. The other? Well. . . .

We start thinking, "Won't it be wonderful to get back to the field so we can take a rest for awhile?" Things begin looking good on the other side of the pond. How are we going to get there? Raise money. Oh, yes, hit the road again! Well, friends, by the time we get back to the field again, we're in need of another furlough. A furlough did I say? Forget it! If that's a rest, what must the work be like? The only chance of getting a rest on your furlough is to plan never to return to the mission field. Then there may be some chance of you being around long enough for the roast beef and the jumping bass.

17. ARMCHAIR GENERALSHIP

The spiritual man judges all things, but is himself to be judged by no one. 'For who has known the mind of the Lord to instruct him?' " — I Corinthians 2:15-16

Not that we venture to class or compare ourselves with some of those who commend themselves. But when they measure themselves by one another, and compare themselves with one another, they are without understanding. — II Corinthians 10:12

"I know you are very busy, but for the good of the work would you please answer the following fifty questions?" Have you received letters like this recently? Some good soul is always trying to analyze missionary work to see what makes it tick. This is the age of computers, statistics, IBM and all that. I don't know about you, but it gives me a charge when the so-called experts miss the boat. I don't mind answering reasonable inquiries by anyone, but I wonder if all of the personality tests, examinations, minute facts, etc. really tell the story. I wouldn't be the least bit surprised if most missionaries flunked a test designed to show who should be and who shouldn't be a missionary. I know the work I am doing wouldn't compare favorably with some of the great things being done by others. It seems to me that the right questions are never asked. They deal with surface things like, How many people this? and How much money that?, and How soon will the work no longer require outside funds? (or, how soon can we get out of supporting missionary work?) Sometimes I get the impression that they want some kind of guarantee that they are supporting the number one team, not number two. Sometimes I feel like returning a questionnaire with inquiries like, "Are you willing to support a work till death do part?" or, "Can you put up with fifty years of failure in order to get a work started?" "Would you be willing to preach to an audience of not more than ten people for five or ten years?" "Would you be willing to work twenty-five years with the methods you recommend?" "Are you?" "Did you?"

I'm still old fashioned enough to believe that there are many things that cannot be measured by tests, and machines, and human brains. A beloved teacher of mine told me, "You cannot take the square root of a poem, or the weight of an idea." This I believe! Can you measure the good that is done? Can we comprehend the love of Christ? Can we instruct the Lord? Can we reach understanding by comparing ourselves with ourselves? Of course not.

Now lest someone accuse me of recommending the status quo, and unwillingness to change, or improve anything, let me say, study! Collect facts! Write questionnaires! Make sober judgments! But do it humbly. Do it spiritually. Do it knowing the measure you measure with shall measure you. Generalship is needed, but not armchair generalship.

An expert toured the mission fields of the world and gave a written analysis of the good points and the bad points of the work he saw. He was kind enough to mention by name the places where he thought all was well, and to omit the names of the missionaries and places where he had some criticism. Some so-called experts aren't even this kind. Anyway, in most cases you can figure out who he was talking about. Let us even admit that the expert's month-long insight was greater than the thirty years' insight of the missionary; still, his judgments must be humble, and temporary, and subject to revisions. How does he know what God might use, and how He might use it? What has he felt with a broken heart there? What has he experienced there with his own sweat and blood? What vision of hope has God given him there in the dark, frustrating days?

I would like to be well thought of. I would like the missionary work I am doing to be also well thought of. But I don't worry about it any more. I will judge all things and be judged of no man. (Now, now, that doesn't mean I'm going to be dogmatic and unreasonable. You see "judging all things" means you are going to consider all things, and be reasonable about all things.) No expert can sit in judgment on the Lord's servant. The Lord has things for me to do that you know not of. The Lord has done things with me, that no man can touch. I don't have to be recommended by anybody, or recommend myself. "For it is not the man who commends himself that is accepted but the man whom the Lord commends."

I think we are all too quick to recommend ourselves through the work we are doing, or attribute to our methods that which may not actually be the case. Like a good missionary, I've turned work over to the natives and seen it fall to pieces, and I've turned work over and seen it go-go-go. There is more involved than meets the eye. There are unseen motives and spiritual forces at work. There is the unseen grace and providence of the Spirit of God working out that which is pleasing to Him. I used to be quick to grab only success for myself, and delegate failure to others. But I am slowly learning that I must also grab failure, and bear it, and wait for the working of God, for perchance God will work through the weakness, and not through the strength. He may choose the methodless, and not the method. He may recommend what is not recommended. So be careful armchair generals, and also be careful battle line commanders, lest you find yourself in the position of instructing God, and recommending yourself to others!

18. FALLING INTO THE GROUND

Truly, truly I say to you, unless a grain of wheat falls into the earth and dies, it remains alone; but if it dies it bears much fruit. He who loves his life loses it, and he who hates his life in this world will keep it for eternal life. If anyone serves me he must follow me, and where I am, there shall my servant be also; if anyone serves me, the Father will honor him.

— JOHN 12:24-26

When I was younger, I had fearful dreams of falling into the earth, but when I began to enjoy these plunges from the heights, fear left me and the nightmares ceased. Following Christ into the mission fields produces similar sensations. We felt like we were losing something, and many times would grasp onto the vestiges of the former life, and make efforts to duplicate it. Visiting Christians would remind us saying, "Aren't you homesick? Don't you miss living in the States?" I repeated these questions to an elderly lady missionary once, and she said, "I am not alone; Jesus is with me. I have a roof over my head; what more do I need?" She had fallen into the ground without fear.

When at our baptism, we were united with Christ in the likeness of His death, our old life of sin was crucified with Him. All of its sins and guilt were removed, and we began a new life. But doesn't that old life keep seeking a comeback? That's why we are told to "Put to death therefore what is earthly in you" (Colossians 3:5). We died with Christ. Therefore, we must keep on dying, as the grain of wheat must keep on falling into the ground and keep on dying. This is what Jesus means when He teaches us to hate our life in this world. But this is where we have a lot of trouble. We want our existence in this world to be recognized. If we are honored and praised, it makes us feel valuable and important. For this reason we do not want to lose those things that make us feel that way. Money, possessions, talents, family, friends, popularity, all make up the life of the world, and all of this is what Jesus calls us to leave behind. To lose yourself in some seemingly God-forsaken place, to let go of all, and fall without fear into the earth, seems to this world a suicidal act, a foolish waste of life. But in reality, it is the opposite, because, unless we let God substitute the life He wants for us, for the life we want for ourselves, His will cannot be done and we cannot be given eternal life. How can we live an *eternal* life if we refuse to fall away from the present life? Following Christ means dying like a grain of wheat, to bring forth fruit like a grain of wheat. There can be no sense of worldly security as one falls to the ground, but there is the joy and exhilaration of being with Christ. There can be no expectation of worldly honor in throwing away your life for Christ, but there is the promise of Christ saying, "If anyone serves me, the Father will honor him." The grain of wheat is lost in the ground. It has fallen out of sight, but it is in the place where God generates life, and produces fruit. Oh Christian missionary of Christ, your work may seem for nought, it may seem a failure, it may seem to be unrecognized, it may seem dead, but this is good, this is God's way, this is seed for the future harvest, this is life eternal. If we die with Him, we shall live with Him. Becoming a missionary to this world meant a death sentence for our Lord. Should it mean any less for us? It also meant an eternal life-sentence for our Lord. Will it mean any less for us? Let me say further, that falling into the ground can mean giving up a religious life that is important to us. It can mean leaving behind an important Kingdom job, a promising preacher's salary, a meeting schedule booked up for five years, a place of continual recognition and honor among God's people. These things can be of utmost importance to you. The ninety and nine can be more important to you than the one. I am sure that our Lord was important in Heaven. I'm sure that there were important things for Him to do there. But all this was left behind when He fell into the earth like a small grain of wheat. He gave up one kind of religious life for another kind. Will it mean any less for us? We can be living a religious life that is important, but too convenient. We can be living a religious life that we have grown up in that is comfortable and nice but involves no sacrifice, no falling into the ground, no dying. Is it possible that we are serving Christ and really we are not? To serve Christ, we must follow Him. Where did He go? Where is He? He has fallen into the ground, and there, and there only is He dying and living. I'm not saying that you have to leave America in order to serve Christ, but that Christ says we must leave self in order to serve Him. If the seed does not die it remains alone, selfish and unfruitful. If it dies it bears fruit. If self is taken out of the picture, then there are no boundaries, no limitations to what we will do or where we will do it for Christ.

19. NO REPORTS, NO MONEY!

Are we beginning to commend ourselves again? Or do we need as some do, letters of recommendation to you or from you? — II CORINTHIANS 3:1

Sound no trumpet before you, as the hypocrites do in the synagogues and in the streets, that they may be praised by men — MATTHEW 6:2

A missionary learns right away that reports must be made to all who contribute to his work. Once in a while missionaries are coached as to how this should be done. "Send them monthly. Make them factual. Make them interesting. Make them inspirational. Justify the money expended. Acknowledge all contributions. Don't make them too long. Don't make them too short. Remember the rules of good communications," etc., etc. I must be a good accomplished author, a certified accountant, a diligent public relations man, a good secretary, and a man with enough leisure time to accomplish this.

Some years ago, a friend of mine told me that his missionary father took a week out of every month to write and run off reports. I hardly believed him then; I heartily believe him now. My hat is off to many of my fellow-missionaries who turn out beautiful, well-written reports month after month. I don't know how they do it. I'm not criticizing; I'm just confessing that I couldn't do it without spending a lot of time, and even then the quality of the job might not be up to par.

I wonder, are we requiring more of the missionary than is reasonable? Is the missionary to hold up the hands of the 200 Christians that are supporting him, or are the 200 Christians to hold up the hands of the missionary? The odds are against one man satisfying 200 people, but in favor of 200 satisfying one. To keep supporting brethren well-informed and happy about a work they are supporting is a monumental task in most cases, but I believe brethren can accomplish the reverse much easier. Missionary workers need the help of many in this problem of good reporting. Many are the missionaries, and many are the hours and days they spend composing and publishing reports.

"No reports, no money!" was the theme of the article I read. True it is, and a terrible reality, especially in light of the fact that to a great extent the missionary finds that with "No money, there is nothing to report." Funds are needed to accomplish the contents of good reports, so the obligation is laid squarely upon the missionary's time and talents not only to report but also to keep his support coming. Again we must realize that if the missionary is to do missionary work he needs the help of the 200. "No money, no reports" would also make a good theme for an article.

Well, "Are we beginning to commend ourselves again?" I hope not. There is, though, another consideration. After all, we are involved in a work of faith. I thank God for the few brethren I know who trust me to do my best and don't have to be coddled by glowing reports, and many thank you's, in order to keep up their contributions. And another thing, too many requirements along the reporting line create an unedifying situation where the only purpose of reporting seems to be to get money. Thus the temptation exists to only write those things that will accomplish this. Letters by Paul to those who supported him show that there are many more things important to the content of a missionary's letter than financial matters only.

I often wonder as I write about the work that I am involved in, whether or not I am "blowing my horn." Are we to work to be seen of men? Are we to write letters to be seen of men? Will the Lord say to us who were diligent to tell all brethren everywhere about our wonderful work, "You have had your reward?" Is there no place for a man of God to quietly go about his task of sowing the seed of the kingdom? Is there no place for brethren to go quietly about supporting their men in the field? Does the left hand have to know what the right hand is doing? Does everybody have to be told about how much somebody is giving? Is getting money so important that we have to sacrifice our reward in Heaven in order to get everyone to know us and think well of our work? Reports must be made, but as there is a way not to do it, there is a way also to do it. We can report with good motives. We do not have to sound a trumpet before us. We do not have to please everybody. We do not have to have all the money we want. We do not have to magnify ourselves. We can give glory to our Lord, without whom all our reporting is hot air, and all our money is valueless, and all our labor is in vain.

20. THE DAY I GAVE THE CHURCH TO CHRIST

And he has put all things under his feet and has made him to be head over all things for the church, which is his body, the fullness of him who fills all in all. — EPHESIANS 1:22-23

I remember the day very clearly. I was on my way to my office. My heart was burdened down to the ground. The work I had done at Hitachi was coming apart at the seams. Dissensions, trouble, criticism and all of those things that go with a bad church situation. The devil was having a field day. I thought, "I did this, when I should have done that. I need to. . . . I should have. . . . I will. . . . I can't. . . . I. . . . I. . . . I. . . ." Then it struck me like a bolt out of the blue. Too much I and not enough of Christ. I had preached the above Scripture many times, but I had never allowed it to be practiced by myself. I was acting like the church belonged to me. Does not the church belong to Christ? Is not Christ the head of this church? Am I seeking His will or mine? My critics had called me "The Pope of Hitachi," but I felt that the criticism was not worthy of attention. But now, what about it? Wasn't I worrying like the church was all mine? Wasn't I trying to solve things by my own thoughts and edicts? Yes, I was! "Oh Christ! Thy will be done." I gave the church back to Christ.

What a burden was lifted from my heart. I skipped and leaped with happiness. I still had to face the problems, but now *we* faced them. Christ and I. That made a difference. If I had let Christ have His own way in the first place, and had not been so paternalistic in relations with the brethren in the second place, the problems might not have become so bad in the third place. I had started learning a lesson that all missionary workers need to learn. The church is the Lord's, and the brethren are His. We missionaries tend to run everything and control everything and this leaves no room for the working of the Lord. We lay our plans to do this, and direct that, and dominate the native brethren to the point that Christ has no room to work in them either. Christ is "head over all things for the church," not the missionary, nor the native brethren either. They must learn, also, that the church is His body, and they will learn sooner if we will give the church back to Christ, and take our humble places as servants of Him, and fellow-workers with our brethren.

21. THOSE LAZY MISSIONARY WIVES!

And the twelve were with him, and also some women. . . . — LUKE 8:1-2
Help these women, for they have labored side by side with me in the gospel. . . . — PHILIPPIANS 4:3

Once in Japan, a famous visitor came by to visit the work being done at Ibaraki Christian College and its vicinity. She was shocked by what she found. Her conversations with the wives of the missionaries there revealed that some of these women were not teaching classes, they were not out at night teaching and working with their husbands. In fact, they were not even teaching many classes in the school. The report was taken back to the United States, and at the largest Lectureship in our brotherhood it was stated that the missionary wives in Ibaraki were not helping their husbands, and were in fact, lazy. A fine couple who were considering going to work in Ibaraki came to my home highly disturbed by the report.

Well, I guess it is possible for a missionary wife to be lazy if she works at it hard enough. Even though we teach that wives should be "workers at home (Titus 2:5), and "rule well the household (I Timothy 5:14), some folks are irritated when they see others doing it. We have the idea that a woman must have a career outside the home or she stifles her personality and all that. I don't believe it. Some recreation? Yes. A career? No. The Bible says a double-minded man is "unstable in all his ways (James 1:7-8). Well, it goes for a woman too. If you want instability in the personalities of the children and husbands and wives, then take most wives out of their homes and give them another career. Listen, God's way is best. You'd better believe it!

Home is a happy refuge, not a lonely motel. A bright and cheerful home is essential to the mental and spiritual health of a missionary and his family. This is emphasized exceedingly when working in a foreign land. I know of missionaries who made their home Grand Central Station. They were always worn out, their nerves always on edge. Others made it an office and a meeting place, and where did they go for peace and quiet? Away from home! They went out to visit a home where there was some family atmosphere! When things go wrong in the work, and the pressures are great, home is where you catch your balance, where your happiness is regained.

Concerning those wives in Ibaraki, by doing the work of faithful wives they were making possible the vigorous, dedicated efforts of their husbands. They were a part of everything their husbands did. I will not repeat here what it takes to make a successful wife and mother, but I do want to add that missionary wives face problems on the foreign field that most women nowadays never dream of. Shall I mention that many have to teach their own children through at least eight grades (if they last on mission fields that long)? They have to make heroic efforts to overcome language barriers, loneliness, lack of medical facilities, and sometimes a very ignorant and very heathen society in which their children are being raised. A lazy missionary wife? Unheard of!

I remember some visitors came by once and all the women took time out from their various duties to have a pleasant chat and coffee with them. Later, the report came back that the critics had concluded that all the wives did was to sit around playing and drinking coffee all day! It seems that some people get a thrill at finding something critical to say about missionaries.

Some have been disillusioned and even angered to find out that missionaries and their wives live like ordinary human beings if possible. To some, it is a crime unforgivable if the missionary should have something in his home that the critic doesn't have. Well, there is one thing that I am determined to keep in my home and that's a wife and mother. I'm sure the time comes when, with children raised and God-given duties accomplished, a woman can participate in more outside activities. But let us not frustrate good women who are loyally doing what God called them to do as wives and mothers by demanding they neglect this to follow a "religious career." Hats off to those hard working pioneer wives who are backing up their missionary husbands in the great and good work of preaching the gospel. And missionary wives, be satisfied that you are doing the will of the Lord when you work at being a wife and a mother.

22. HOW TO STAY ALIVE ON THE FIELD

But we will devote ourselves to prayer and to the ministry of the word. — ACTS 6:4

If anyone does not provide for his relatives, and especially for his own family, he has disowned the faith. . . . — 1 TIMOTHY 5:8

Let us look at two missionaries. The first thinks, "I've got to fix that thing again. I must write a letter. There is shopping to do. I'll pick up the mail. I'll go see what so and so is doing. I'll pick up the kids. I'll work on the report. Oh, so much to do and so little time to do it!" A second one thinks, "I've got six classes to teach today. I must stop by the hospital. I'll squeeze in a church business meeting. I have to counsel brother so and so. I've got to get ready for the meeting that begins tomorrow. Oh, so much to do and so little time to do it!" Which of these two is doing the will of the Lord? The answer is easy, of course: neither of them, and both of them! The "neither of them" answer: The first one is spending his time dominated by trivia. He is filling his hours with frustrating, unending details of life, and neglecting the mission God has given him to accomplish. The second is too busy for his own good, and for the good of his family. He is neglecting the necessary details of the human life God has given us to live. The "both of them" answer: The first one is doing God's will by taking care of his responsibilities as a husband and father. The second one is deeply involved in the work that God has given preachers to do.

If the two missionaries continue with every day typical of the above, who will last the longest? Well, all things being equal, neither of them. The first one will frustrate himself continually, not finding enough time to do the work of a missionary, and will become discouraged and give it up. The second one is so intense at his mission that he will soon be frustrated by a neglected family, and a tired, nervous body.

This brings us to four recommendations that I believe will keep the missionary alive and healthy and working a long time in the field he has chosen.

1. Take time for devotions. Each day should begin, continue and end with prayer and meditation. Notice that prayer preceded the ministry of the Word. How can we work for the Lord without calling upon Him for guidance? The pitfalls of trivia and overwork can be avoided by good communications with God. We are balanced up and kept from extremes by prayer and Bible reading every day.

2. Don't be afraid *not* to work. Conscience is a guide, not a

slavedriver. It is contrary to the will of God to feel that you should be working all the time. We need to see Christ asleep in the boat, and hear Him say, "Come away by yourselves to a lonely place and rest awhile (Mark 6:31). You must take time out from your round of activities to relax and care for the body and mind that God has given you to use.

3. Don't persecute your family. This is done when you work too much and find yourself out of joint with the more leisurely pace a family takes. Getting into a temper and taking your frustrations out on your children or wife will guarantee a short term on the field and a long furlough in the States. If you consider the affairs of your family an interruption of your work, you are sinning for not being willing to be the husband and father that you chose to be, and that God made you to be. The work of the Lord involves more than just preaching and teaching.

4. Do what you were sent to do. There is no way of avoiding the details of life, and the many interruptions that occur, but you need to organize your activities, and make sure that you accomplish the teaching and preaching that is the essential life of being a missionary. Make sure you are doing what God sent you to do. This will keep you happy in your work. But if you get involved in non-related matters, or get jobs stacked on you that keep you from your missionary endeavor, you will suffer great dissatisfaction and find that the only way to get rid of it is to get rid of the field you are working in. Staying alive on the field, and staying a long time is absolutely essential to the sowing and harvesting that our Lord has called us to do. Let's stay on the field, and stay alive on the field!

23. HEART TROUBLE AND LIFE EXPECTANCY

For we do not want you to be ignorant, brethren, of the affliction we experienced in Asia; for we were so utterly unbearably crushed that we despaired of life itself. — II CORINTHIANS 1:8

49

*For I wrote you out of much affliction and anguish
of heart and with many tears. . . .*
    — II CORINTHIANS 2:4

*As commissioned by God. . . . Such is the confidence
that we have. . . . Since we have such a hope we
are very bold. . . . So we do not lose heart. . . . So
we are always of good courage. . . .*
    — II CORINTHIANS 2:17; 3:4, 12; 4:16; 5:6

Why do some missionaries quit and go home? Why do some
stay on? Without giving the impression that I know all about
these matters, I do feel compelled to say something. A good
reason is always given for leaving the mission field. I've never
heard a poor one yet. Brethren who have never left jobs, homes
and the like to serve Christ in a strange place will always
understand why one returns home. But what happened? What
changed the dedicated, zealous, outgoing missionary into a spir-
itless, discouraged, incoming-ex-missionary? Would it be too
great a generalization to say heart trouble? Heart trouble and a
limited life-expectancy go hand in hand. A heart attack can
paralyze and bring to a cessation all work. Although there may
be other reasons needful of consideration, I consider heart trouble the greatest cause of the high missionary mortality rate.

What happened to the heart? What knocked the mission out
of the missionary? The mission was to preach the gospel to lost
souls. Are there now no longer any lost souls? If the desire to
preach is gone, has faith been replaced by unbelief? Has some
terrible lethargy settled upon the missionary's heart? This can
happen. The unbelief and disobedience of a heathen society can
rub off on the missionary. It can corrode and dull the sense of
urgency to save lost souls. It can disappoint and disillusion the
sincere heart. It can cause heart trouble of various kinds.

It could be that the ex-missionary found the going too rough.
The many barriers to be overcome, the stresses and strains upon
his family, his health, his patience — all of these affect the fixed
determination of the missionary. If his heart is moved by these,
then he is in danger of losing his mission. If his heart remains
true to his calling, then there are ways to overcome the difficul-

ties, the barriers can be surmounted, the machinations of Satan can be defeated.

Is it not love that keeps the mssionary heart ticking? Is not the heart gone out of everything when the love is lost? To no longer love the people one is working among, is to no longer be a missionary. Love covers a multitude of irritations, frustrations, and setbacks. It was the love of lost souls that moved one to become a missionary for Christ. It makes one heartsick to find out that he is empty of love for lost souls. It is shocking indeed. It means a rethinking of one's whole Christian life. You don't have to leave home to find this out. You don't have to leave a mission field when you find it out. It can be cured.

What is the remedy for heart trouble? A new heart, a renewed dedication. What kept Paul and his fellow-workers going on the mission fields? The above Scriptures show that they did not avoid afflictions and anguish of heart. But they also show that they did not lose heart either. They remembered their commission from God. They realized once more what they were called to do. They did not let anything keep them from fulfilling their mission.

If we are to improve the life-expectancy of the missionary, we must give attention first and foremost to his heart. You can study all the anthropology, culture, language, and mission methods that there are, but when the heart collapses, everything collapses. We must go forth with strong hearts. We must not lose these hearts. These hearts must be filled with the love of God for lost souls. They must be trained in the grace and love of Christ. Then, and only then, will hearts not fail in the missions that God gives them to perform.

24. EXES

But they all alike began to make excuses. . . .
— LUKE 14:18

Take care, brethren, lest there be in any of you an evil, unbelieving heart, leading you to fall away from the living God. — HEBREWS 3:12

Somewhere I saw statistics that show we now have twice as many ex-missionaries as we have the other kind. This is sad, but apparently true. I know why many of them returned to their home country, and why they cannot leave it again. We must sympathize, not judge. They have borne burdens from which most brethren have turned aside. They have broken their hearts and their health on a cross of self-sacrifice, and remain a living reminder of the price that some pay to take the gospel of Christ to foreign lands.

At the same time, we must give consideration to what makes an ex-missionary. There is something to be learned, some warnings to be heeded. Though some may have "good" reasons for not continuing on, and God's will for one, may not be His will for another, still we must face the possibility that a man or woman may quit the field because of unbelief. If a missionary loses his mission, he may lose his faith. Is not his mission to preach the gospel in order that lost souls might be saved? What if he now considers this mission an impossibility for himself and for others? Could he not try to justify aborting his mission by saying because man cannot do the job, God in the end will save everyone anyway? This liberal theological view is held by quite a few in the religious world. It is in reality though, a position of unbelief. The Word of God declares that the world is lost, not seemingly lost, to be actually saved in the judgment day. Also it teaches that the believing are not seemingly saved to be actually lost in the judgment day. One can quit the field feeling that in some way or another God will save everybody in the judgment whether the gospel is preached to them or not. In unbelief of God's Word, we think that unbelievers will be saved in their unbelief of God's Word. This will not do.

One can become an ex-missionary by feeling that somebody else can do the suffering necessary to getting the mission done. This they accomplish immediately by their departure, for many are the responsibilities they leave behind for others to bear. But again, I want to say that this feeling is unbelief. You see, the mission of the missionary is shared by all Christians. Now, you can become an ex-missionary, but if you become missionless you become an ex-Christian. Christ said, "If any man would come after me, let him deny himself, take up his cross daily and follow me" (Luke 9:23). You cannot be a Christian and not bear the suffering, sacrifice and responsibilities of a cross. If we are followers of Christ, we must share in the mission of His cross wherever we may be. If you are missionless, you are crossless and Christless. Every Christian shares in the mission of saving lost souls. We are faithless when we refuse to do this. Is it possible that the churches are full of ex-Christians dwelling in an unbelief that caused them to cease the suffering and inconvenience of the mission to save lost souls?

It could be God's will that causes one to become an ex-missionary, but it is not God's will that we become missionless. It may be God's will that we not leave home for work in foreign lands, but it is not God's will that we should be missionless, lest we become Christless, ex-Christians.

How can you explain ex-missionaries who no longer have an active interest in the field where they labored? If their conscience is now dead concerning mission work, can it be because they are now missionless? Is not this unbelief? Is not this unbelief shared by all who live without concern for the lost, whether at home or abroad? I thank God for those ex-missionaries who are not missionless, who have not forgotten what God called them to do, and who are working with all of their might to teach others and stir them up to accomplish the Christian's worldwide mission.

I am convinced that some become ex-missionaries for the same reason some refuse the mission of the cross. I know one can become tired of the burdens, tired of doing without, tired of shabby treatment, and feel like "I'm not going to suffer any more; I'm going to take care of myself." But at this juncture couldn't we be saying that "I'm tired of doing the will of Christ. I'm going to do my own will from now on?" Is it not this disobedient attitude of brethren that keeps them from sharing in the mission of saving souls in the first place? Do we want to be numbered among them? God forbid. Let us fulfill the mission of our Lord anywhere we go. Let us be willing to pay the price of sacrifice and suffering, and so share in the cross of Christ, that we may also share in the eternal life of His resurrection.

25. JACK OF ALL TRADES, MASTER OF NONE

Show yourself in all respects a model of good deeds.
— TITUS 2:7

Do this work of an evangelist, fulfill your ministry.
— II TIMOTHY 4:5

What is a missionary? What is he supposed to do? I have never met a missionary that wasn't an astute juggler of many balls, a switch hitter who played all the positions, a chameleon called upon to reflect every situation, a variety store, a mulligan stew, a strange mixture of heaven and earth. Think of what a missionary is called upon to do, and what he does. He is a financier, a public relations man, a fund raiser. He must be an educator, a personnel director, an able administrator. He must be a linguist, a translator, interpreter, author, and publisher. He must be a practicing physician, nurse and first aid man, a counselor, anthropologist, and sociologist. He is expected to be an English language expert, an ambassador of his country, to have a keen insight into national and international politics, and always be able to take the right position on any problem that arises. He is a philanthropist, organizer and operator of benevolent institutions, a lecturer, orator, and teacher of many things. We might add that he preaches the gospel once in a while, too!

We have a saying, "Circumstances alter cases," and this aptly applies to the role of the missionary. The missionary's own background, education and inclination effect his role. What a missionary does and can do is determined, also, by how old he is, how long he has been on the field, the educational level of a people, the climate of the country, the economic level of its society and the political stability of an area. All are factors that influence the work of a missionary.

A changing world can mean a changing role for the missionary. But there is one trade the missionary must be master of to deserve the name. I want to emphasize that the missionary is primarily a gospel preacher, a bearer of good news. His work is to save souls. There should be only one mission for his life, one role that must supersede all others, in order to be worthy of the name "missionary." This is the unchanging role assigned by the Great Commission, "Go ye into all the world and preach the gospel. . . ."

In too many cases, the missionary becomes a Martha, troubled and worried about many things. He needs to hear the Lord when He says, "Only one thing is needful," and like Mary, choose the better part. Though he may be busy doing many good things, if he fails to proclaim the gospel, he will see fruit without a tree, light without a sun, water without a source, and chaff without wheat. The winds of change will blow and nothing will remain. His field of many labors will be a valley of dry bones. He will have failed because, among the accumulated wares of a life with many roles, he will have left dust-covered, and neglected, the most important role of all — his mission to seek and save the lost.

26. DEAR JOHN

What you would have gained from it is given to God.
— MATTHEW 15:5

No church entered into partnership with me in giving and receiving except you only; for even in Thessalonica you sent me help once and again.
— PHILIPPIANS 4:15-16

"We regret to inform you that due to local needs we will terminate our support of your work commencing January first." Is there a missionary that has never received a letter like this? I believe most of us have received more than one. These are "Dear John" letters telling us that they don't love us any more. These letters used to arrive like bombshells, ripping the family budget to shreds, and upsetting our spirits, until we learned to put more faith in God than in men. As long as the Lord is feeding the sparrows, we will be taken care of. When the birds stop eating, missionaries will become extinct.

You would be surprised how irresponsible some churches can

be! I know of a preacher who was "forgotten." The church changed treasurers and the new man forgot to send the checks. The preacher was dropped without a word, 8,000 miles away. He died a bitter man. Another man arrived on the field and didn't get any support for three months. The church didn't know how to send the money! There is no defense against these practices except the dedication of the one who is dumped. In most cases I know of, no notice is given. In December you are told that funds will cease in January. That's all, brother!

This is no way to conduct the work of the Lord! The tragedy of it is that such a church is not only inconsiderate of the man they are supporting, but it is also callous to the harm that is done to the work. More than once the carelessness of a supporting church has robbed a missionary of a month's salary. It happens when checks that come at the end of the month start coming at the first of the next month and then slip to the end of that month. This keeps the man in debt and constantly borrowing to make ends meet. Are these isolated cases? I wish they were. Missionaries seldom complain about these practices. Most of the men are insensitive about money matters, and are willing to sacrifice to serve the Lord. But this does not justify their fellow Christians taking advantage of this to buy labor cheap. It does not justify the shabby treatment given to men of God. A real preacher and a real missionary is going to go on with his task regardless of how he is treated. We are not hirelings! But it does remind me somewhat of the practice of corban among the Jews. Christ referred to it in the preceding Scripture verses — a Jew could be freed from the obligation of supporting his parents if he made a contribution to the temple. In this way the word of God was thwarted by a contribution to God. Recently, support was cut off from a missionary because the money was needed to pay off the debt on a church building. "It was given to God." How much support has not gone to mission fields because of the debts accrued in the construction of "temples." I know a fine couple who spent a year trying to raise passage to get to a mission field. I don't know whether they will get back at the needed time or not. Like many of us they will have to borrow money in order to accomplish it.

I shouldn't finish this chapter without a salute to the faithful, considerate supporters who are seeing that the lines of supply and communication are kept up all over the world, that the men they support may carry on the great task of preaching the gospel to every creature. The church at Philippi was that kind of church. It is implied by Paul that other churches should have backed him up in his mission work, but that only Philippi did. This was to their honor and the glory of God.

We are in the most important work in the world. If companies, governments and armies conducted their affairs like some of us do they would be out of business pronto. To. the best of our ability let us see that a good job is done for our Lord in the mission fields of the world.

27. HOW MANY MISSIONARIES DO WE NEED?

Sopater of Beroea, the son of Pyrrhus, accompanied him; and of the Thessalonians, Aristarchus and Secundus; and Gaius of Derbe, and Timothy; and the Asians, Tychicus and Trophimus. — ACTS 20:4

A famous Christian in the church said, "It is impossible for us to send enough missionaries to do the enormous task of evangelizing the world." I don't agree with him, but as long as our faith is lacking we are going to have to learn to get along without reinforcements. We decided a long time ago that if we were going to get the job of evangelization done in Japan, it would have to be without the help of more missionaries. Doesn't every overloaded missionary in every clime face the reality of a lack of personnel to get the job done? How many opportunities to save souls were lost because no worker was available?

Someone said we now have over 200 missionaries in the various fields of the world. Well, we had that many ten years ago. One good brother has almost doubled the number by counting the wives of missionaries. That's okay because these women are a part of the work, but I always counted a husband and wife as one body. In all the statistics that I have seen, I have never seen workers who were not Americans, or Canadians, counted as missionaries. We seem to think, that missionary work can only be done by officially titled and recognized *Missionaries,* when in reality the best and most permanent job of missionary work is being done by the nationals themselves. I work more or less directly with twelve national preachers. This is true of many missionaries, so we could increase the statistics at least ten times, and if we included their wives it would be twenty times. This would give us a more solid number to consider.

You will notice that Paul's fellow-missionaries were natives of the various regions where he had been preaching the gospel. They were not all Jews from his hometown of Tarsus, or his home country of Judea. The fact that they were not Jews did not make them any less missionaries for Christ. If we are going to get the job of evangelization done, we should use the missionary potential of the countries in which we are working. Must we always look for an American to send into a strange land? Should not the workers in the mission fields of all the world be encouraged to take the gospel to neighboring countries also?

Another thing, are not all Christians missionaries for Christ? Does not the entire membership of the Christian churches around the world represent the true potential for evangelization? Should not programs be developed that would inspire and encourage them to do more missionary work? If we "go with what we've got," we can evangelize the world in our generation, and in every generation to come. What about it? How many missionaries do we need? We have enough to start with. Let's use what we have and the grace of God will give us whatever else we need. How about it?

28. I'LL NEVER MAKE THAT MISTAKE AGAIN!

Did I not choose you, the twelve, and one of you is a devil? — JOHN 6:70

Demas forsook me, having loved this present world.
— II TIMOTHY 4:10

They separated from each other; Barnabas took Mark with him . . . but Paul chose Silas and departed.
— ACTS 15:39-40

We learn by experience, but that does not mean that we should stop experiencing what we learn. It is true and wise for us to avoid making the same mistake twice, but to remove the possibility of ever making the same mistake again, can be the greatest mistake ever. In order to do a good job at anything we must take the risk of sometimes doing a poor job. In working with people you must trust them, but there exists the possibility that one of them may be untrustworthy. When this occurs it would really be a mistake to say, "I will never trust anyone again!" To experience betrayal is unpleasant and excruciating. You certainly do not want to go through the experience again! In working with foreign nationals, missionaries have disappointing experiences. Some trusted worker runs off with the money. You find you have swallowed lies hook, line and sinker. Embarrassing isn't it? If we determine that we will never be taken for a ride again, to the extent that we become suspicious of everybody, we make it impossible for anyone to be proved trustworthy. Also, we will find ourselves not loving our fellow-workers, for in loving, there is trusting.

I'm not saying that we should be blind to what is happening. It seems that the Lord put up with Judas for the sake of the others, even when He knew what Judas was going to do. We do not know who will turn out to be a crook or an immoral person and yet we are called upon to trust our fellow-laborers. Paul was not able to avoid the pitfalls of choosing a companion who turned out wrong. It is hard for us to forget the shame of having been fooled by someone, but we should not be sissies about it. We must be willing, like our Lord and His apostles, to take the sins and weaknesses of others to our bosoms, even though it means a shameful cross to bear. Only in this way will the untrustworthy learn trustworthiness, and only in this way will those who are worthy be seen as worthy. If we withdraw in fears and doubts to protect ourselves from suffering, we will never know who is true to the Lord, and we will never make a real friend. Some missionaries will chop off a native worker the first time he makes a mistake in order to protect himself or his money. Others will refrain from giving native Christians responsibilities that carry the possibility of betrayal. When the Lord knew Judas was going to betray Him for money, why did He allow him to continue as keeper of the moneybox? Think about it!

Now Paul and Barnabas fought over Mark because he had deserted them on their first missionary journey. Paul didn't want to trust him on the second journey, but Barnabas did. Well, it turned out all right. Mark had learned his lesson and proved to be a faithful and valuable worker. Later Paul welcomed him and commended him as a fellow missionary (II Timothy 4:11). But somebody trusted the untrusted Mark again, and this trust was rewarded. Paul didn't want to make the same mistake twice it seems.

Do not make the mistake of being afraid to make mistakes. I'm not commending mistakes, but I am commending the grace of Christ that can bring out of our blunders a good thing. There is no way in the world you can train future missionaries to never make mistakes, but there is a way to train them to put up with their own mistakes and the mistakes of others in order for patience, and the grace of God to have its perfect work. Love must be willing to put up with the same mistake again!

29. THE RICH AMERICAN MISSIONARY

For I have learned, in whatever state I am, to be content. . . . and I know how to abound . . . I have learned the secret of facing plenty . . . abundance. . . . I can do all things in him who strengthens me — PHILIPPIANS 4:11-13

Most people think that money will solve all of their problems. To become a rich man is the great ambition of this world. Someone said that there are just as many problems on the other side of riches as there are on this side. How true it is!

Before I became a missionary, I always considered myself an average Joe with middle class ways. I came from a family that lived next to poverty. But what happened when I arrived on the mission field? Suddenly I became a rich Yankee missionary, not in my own eyes, nor in the eyes of those who sent me, but in the eyes of the war-stricken, poverty-stricken nationals among whom we began living. We missionaries were considered Rocke-fellers with unlimited financial resources at our beck and call.

What a shock this was. Some call it "culture shock." I re-member one of my fellow missionaries, whose conscience was reeling at the material difference between himself and the na-tives, trying to explain while preaching a sermon, that he was just a plain country boy. Unfortunately, his new suit, gold ring, and brand new car belied his explanation in the eyes of the audience.

Until becoming a missionary, I had always applied Scrip-ture that dealt with riches and rich men to other people, but now I found to my amazement, that among our fellow Christians on the field, they applied to missionaries first and foremost. In other words, I was the camel that had to get through the eye of a needle. In fact, a world view showed that most North Americans were the rich men of the world!

Our thinking had to be overhauled, and we had to face up to the challenge of "plenty . . . abundance." Paul the missionary also had times and situations where he had to learn how to be a rich missionary. He learned the secret of plenty. He learned how to accept and use abundance, how to be content in every situation.

Some missionaries never get over the social and financial dif-ferences they find on a foreign field. Some are so sensitive about it that they try to effect a radical change in their standard of living and endanger physical, mental, and spiritual health. Guilt feelings about having money and things that others around don't have, discourage and frustrate them. In many instances, money is given away, or spent unwisely. Normal desires of wives and children are resented and tensions build up. Their situation becomes unbearable. Financial differences influence the work the missionary performs. He finds himself an employer respon-sible for the wages and livelihood of others. His mission as a missionary comes under suspicion. Once when visiting a country of the Far East, the native brethren criticized their missionary to me saying, "All he is here for is to make money, else why all the possessions and income?"

The American missionary must learn how to preach the gos-pel, as a rich man. To try to pretend to be what you are not is wrong. He must accept his lot as a foreigner, and as a rich foreigner. He must learn how to use what he is, and what he has, to the glory of God. He must learn to be content, or he will crack under the pressures and retreat to his homeland. We cannot help it if our country is well off. What we can help though, is our attitude toward those less fortunate than we are, and our use of what we have for those less fortunate than we are. Herein is the secret of facing plenty.

I found out that I couldn't change my foreign-looking face, that the people put me in a certain category whether I belonged there or not. When we first went to Japan, I took my old CCM bicycle along. It was made different than Japanese bicycles, so it became the center of many oohs and aahs. They thought it was a wonderful, new kind of bicycle. I finally got tired of the old thing and bought a new Japanese bicycle which was really much better. I couldn't convince them though that my old bike was no good.

In dealing with this problem of differences, I have found out that if you will act without prejudice, if you will eat with them, sympathize with them, and do your best for them, they will accept you as you are, and will give ear to what you say. But if you are arrogant, touchy, bossy or rude, they will resent you for what you are. We must work to preach Christ in spite of our differences. We must learn to use the situations of life that we find ourselves in, to the glory of God. Rich American missionary, make the best of it for the sake of our God.

30. HE WAS A GOOD MISSIONARY NEXT YEAR

I am nothing. — II CORINTIHANS 12:11

I will boast of the things that show my weaknesses.
— II CORINTHIANS 11:30

This is what they should write on my tombstone. Anything else would not represent the facts of my missionary life correctly. I thought I knew a lot of things about missionary work when we first started into it, but those days have gone forever. I'm one of those fellows that makes New Year's resolutions. I do this after some reflection on the previous year, and my conclusion is always the same. That is, "This year I will really do this missionary business right!" My reflections reveal the mistakes I made that I won't make again, and I treasure the many lessons learned. But every year is different. New and valuable lessons are learned, and I guess quite a few forgotten too. When we were five years on the field, I said, "It takes five years to make a missionary." Then after ten years, I said, ten years. Now after twenty, I'm still looking forward to qualifying.

Someone says, "You've been on the field a long time, and it's nice to see that you are humble about it." Well, I am kind of proud of humility, but being humble is of no special merit. The facts in the case compel us to realize that we squeaked through the year by the great grace of Christ. Really, everyone is of humble estate, and to recognize it and confess it is nothing. It is because we have such an exalted view of ourselves that humility is recommended to us as a virtue.

When I think of the mistakes I made last year, and the mistakes I would have made if it hadn't been for Christ, I have to be humble, which is nothing to brag about. I'm glad some of my fellow Christians honor missionaries. Some in fact, think we are saints of a sort in some special way. This is not true, of course, and the wrong impression is given. When admirers find out that there is nothing so special about us, they can become quite disillusioned and disappointed. They should not have been so worshipful in the first place, but we thank them for their good intentions.

If every year continues like the past ones have, we are going to reach the end of the line half-baked in all ways. If it is the grace of Christ that is causing our work to go on, if it is the grace of Christ teaching us how to be missionaries for Him, isn't this a poor comment on us? Doesn't it show that we don't have very much on the ball? Doesn't it mean that we are "unprofitable servants?" Yet this is the case. We are. We must admit it. In spite of the glowing reports, the thrilling biographies, the banquets, the awards. Didn't Christ say to us in Luke 17: 10, "So you also, when you have done all that is commanded you, say, 'We are unworthy servants; we have only done what was our duty?'" Some people are outstanding because they are compared to others, but when they are compared to our Lord, their glory fades. Paul said that people who compare themselves with themselves are ignorant (II Corinthians 10:12). This is true. The more you get to know missionaries and their problems, the more you wonder how anything could get done. You wonder why God put the treasure of the gospel in earthen vessels in the first place. But we know that the foolishness of God is wiser than our wisdom, for the grace of Christ, and the glory of God can be seen clearly to be grace and glory when His will is accomplished through weak vessels. God did not commit the gospel to us to be preached because we would do such a wonderful job of it. Quite the contrary. He chose us because we are really weak, to show that He is really strong. He chose us because we are nothing, to show that His grace is something. For this reason we can all rejoice, and be encouraged to continue, because His grace is upon us to accomplish, in spite of our mistakes and weaknesses, another glorious year of missionary work.

31. ABOUT SPEAKING IN TONGUES

Even if I am unskilled in speaking. . . .
— II Corinthians 11:6

"The most important thing that you can do is learn the language," the new missionary is always told. With this advice, I agree. I have dished it out enough times to know. I also know that the advice is not kept very well. It doesn't take long for the new worker to get involved in this, that and the other, and pretty soon language study becomes a missionary's sideline. To some extent, this cannot be helped. If your brain is the ordinary type, it doesn't take much time to get fed all the language you can digest. In my limited experience, the language was mastered not by those whose scholarly abilities kept up a grueling study every day, but by those who got out among the people and found uses for what they had studied. Too much language, too soon, can be a very discouraging experience. You get what is called among Japan hands, a "Japanese head." This is a kind of sickness where the head swells up and becomes sore due to all the grammar and vocabulary that has been stuffed into it.

I think it is important that language study be enjoyed and useful. This means that there should be a proper proportion of book learning and practical usage. It is strange but true, that it is not always the smart folks that get the language. Scholars are sometimes perfectionists, and they are not willing to go through the childish mistakes and embarrassment necessary to learning a foreign tongue. One must become a baby, a little child, with lisps and stutters, willing to be laughed at when a humorous error is made, willing to go through the monotony and humility of numerous repetitions and corrections.

Another thing. You can't take yourself too seriously when you are learning a language. It can grate on the nerves to have someone giggle during your prayer, or slyly grin during a sermon. But one has to appreciate the humor of the difference a mistake in pronunciation can make between saying "Deny yourself and become a child of God" and "Throw away your pants, and become the son of a turtle." A people instinctively appreciate the efforts of one trying to learn their language, and their laughter is never one of derision. Laugh with them, and learn with them.

I hated languages in school, and always sought ways to get around them. When I thought about becoming a missionary, this was a stumbling block to me. But I concluded, that if God wanted me to become a missionary He would help me do everything essential to being one. Many were the days I sat down in front of the language textbook and prayed, "Lord, help this ignoramus preach in this difficult tongue."

Have you ever heard some foreigner learning English? What a slaughter, eh? How many jokes and imitations do we have about the mispronunciations of English by first generation immigrants? Well, this is how the missionary sounds, and sometimes he sounds that way all of his missionary life. How would you like to hear sermons in the Swedish- or Italian-English dialects? Yet this is what happens when the missionary preaches Christ in a language not his own.

It seems that Paul's Greek was not so hot. Much better than my Greek for sure, but this did not keep him from proclaiming Christ right there in Greece. His lack of skill in the language did not keep him from being a missionary. There were those with whom he worked that knew Greek as their mother tongue. I know some old-time missionaries, who are not language scholars, but they are doing great works for Christ. All the language ability in the world means nothing without the dedication, and earnestness that keeps those missionaries on the job. Language is a barrier, but there is more than one way of overcoming it.

32. ASK NO QUESTIONS FOR STOMACH'S SAKE

For everything created by God is good, and nothing is to be rejected if it is received with thanksgiving.
— I TIMOTHY 4:5

Are you fussy about food? I never thought I was until I got to the Orient. They eat stuff there that you have never even heard of. Worse than that, they eat stuff you have heard of, but never would eat. I remember, not with pride, my first Japanese feast. It looked beautiful, it must have been delicious, but I could hardly stand it. I had trouble even eating rice. I was a roast beef and potato man.

Our hospitable Japanese friends had us over to their house to eat on many occasions. I'm sure that one of the qualifications of a preacher must be his ability to eat. Anyway, as soon as we returned home, it was seltzers and stomach powders for us. For the first time in our lives, we had to study how to eat. First, we would skip the meal preceding the feast in order to guarantee an appetite. Then we would eat a lot of those things we found palatable, and compliment our host and hostess about them. I was brought up to clean my plate always, so when no one was looking, I'd slip what I couldn't stomach into a pocket that I had prepared with tissue or other wrappings. I soon got the reputation of being a great eater of Japanese food!

We soon found out though, that people do not eat that which doesn't taste good. Because of our narrow background in eating habits, only a few things are delicious to most of us. We had to learn to eat Oriental food. By experimenting and trying our best we found many things we liked and learned to tolerate many things that we hated. In fact, after a while, even that which was hated was discovered to be delicious!

Eating everything is very important to being a good missionary. If you worked hard preparing a meal, and your guest refused to eat it, or picked at it like it was poisonous, how would you feel? When we learn to eat with our native friends and brothers, we get close to their hearts. Is not the way to a man's heart through his stomach? I had to make eating a matter of prayer. I had to ask the Lord to help make me be thankful for what I was about to eat.

When I went to Korea, the brethren there gave me fifteen welcome feasts! At first they thought I wouldn't eat Korean food. But when they saw that I would, they stuffed me with it. How could I refuse? It was during war time, and things were hard to get. They paid a lot in the black market to get the food for me. The first few meals I could hardly stand, but after that, I again reached the conclusion that "everything created by God is good, and nothing is to be rejected." There is a price to pay in becoming one with the people you want to save. There are risks involved. But for Christ's sake, it is worth it. When we ate with our poor brethren who lived in the caves of Hitachi, we had some stomach upsets, but the rewards of seeing them come to Christ far outweighed any personal inconvenience. Our bodies are tougher than we think, and they can adjust to many circumstances. If eating with the natives is a problem for you, remember the words of our brother missionary Paul when he said, "Take your share of suffering as a good soldier of Jesus Christ" (II Timothy 2:3). How hard it must have been for Paul to learn to eat with the Gentiles after his training by the Pharisees. They were fussy about foods, cleanliness, etc. Yet in spite of this, he overcame his Jewish training and personal prejudices in order not to be a stumbling block to the Gentiles, in order to proclaim to them the unsearchable riches of Christ.

33. FIRST, BE LAZY!

And what you have heard from me before many witnesses entrust to faithful men who will be able to teach others also. — II Timothy 2:2

This sounds like a good idea. It even sounds easy to do. But you know, this could be the hardest thing a missionary has to learn. Pressures are on the missionary to work, work, work. There is joy in work, and a thrilling sense of accomplishment; but much of the missionary's time is taken up doing jobs that others could do. To a great extent the missionary is on his own when he gets to the field. He makes many decisions by himself. He bears many responsibilities by himself. He becomes very dependent on himself. In other words, it's easy for him to become a "lone wolf." Needless to say, the lone wolf makes a poor leader, and if a missionary needs to be anything, he needs to be a leader,

Paul taught Timothy to be a leader. To train others to teach, that they might teach others to teach. This is the way the gospel is spread. This is the way to get native leadership. This is the way to get native churches to stand on their own feet.

When there is a job to be done, let us first be lazy! Let us see if we can get somebody else to do it. In fact, the missionary's task is to be lazy to the extent of getting everybody else to do everything. When he has accomplished this, he can move on to other places and other work.

It is not easy to entrust important tasks to others because you take the risk of having a poor job done, or having someone fail completely. "If you want a good job done, do it yourself," is a common saying, but it can work you to death. Are jobs more important than people? It is people who need training. We must be willing to put up with half-jobs, and failure can sometimes teach a greater lesson than all the examples of success rolled together.

A missionary asked me once, "How do you get lazy men to work?" There are some people who are really lazy, and if they are workers responsible to you the best thing you can do is fire them. Notice that Paul told Timothy to trust "faithful men." These are men whom you can depend on. Unfaithful men are not to be entrusted with the gospel. But I would like to say, that you find out who is faithful by trial and error. Some can begin lazily and end up a fireball. This means we must be patient with them and put up with their blunders until you can determine the direction in which they are growing. Where there is no growing, no improvement, no fruitbearing, then the axe needs to be laid to the root of the tree.

Many times though, the disgusted missionary goes ahead and does what others should have done. I am not saying that you can completely avoid this kind of thing, but we must first think lazy, asking the questions, Can someone else do this? Who can I get to do it? To multiply yourself as an evangelist and preacher by training others is far superior to doing things yourself. Look around. Involve others in the great mission of Christ. The gospel is not just ours, it is theirs. It is theirs to do with as the Lord directs them. Only when they are trained and trusted, trusted and trained, will the gospel take root in the country where we are laboring.

34. THE CANARY WHO FORGOT ITS SONG

For if I preach the gospel, that gives me no ground for boasting. For necessity is laid upon me. Woe to me if I do not preach the gospel. . . . by all means save some. — I CORINTHIANS 9:16-17, 22

No soldier on service gets himself entangled in civilian pursuits. — II TIMOTHY 2:4

How many kinds of missionaries are there? Well, I know of quite a few. For instance, there are medical missionaries, agricultural missionaries, labor missionaries, administrative missionaries, school teacher missionaries, welfare missionaries, and many others. I suppose this is all right; a good work is a good work. But, you know, I have a feeling that the canary is forgetting to sing. When so-called missionaries are not busy preaching the gospel, I wonder if they have forgotten how? The comeback is, "Well, there is more than one way of preaching the gospel."

Granted. A good example says something, and what I am talking about is the good example of a gospel preacher. The canary can flit around the cage all it wants, but unless it opens its beak and sings, the canary might as well be some other bird.

Missionary life, defined by Paul, means first and foremost, preaching the gospel. He expected a judgment of woe upon himself if he failed to do this. It's easy for a missionary to get off the main track. There are so many needs of all kinds around him — so much to be done, but the whole mission is to preach the gospel and save someone. Some double talkers take "preaching" to mean every kind of work you ever heard of. They also take "salvation" and have it cover every improvement and point of progress from soup to nuts. The New Testament is not vague about what preaching and teaching is, and what the gospel to be taught is, and what the salvation of the soul means.

The big-hearted missionary can get so involved in so many "things" that he fails to accomplish "The Thing," the public and private proclamation of the gospel. I have had the experience of getting so bogged down in school administration or the teaching of English classes, that I had no energy left for anything else. This also is the trouble with a lot of our "approaches." We spend all of our time in "approaching" people that we never do get to them.

Now, soldiers on service for Christ the King should not waste their time in activities that the world carries on, and can carry on without them. Paul's good advice to Timothy needs to be heeded. Soldiers of Christ should not get "entangled in civilian pursuits." Paul "making tents" in Corinth has been used to justify taking flattering positions, and spending time making money in foreign countries. They make it sound like he had a regular tent-making business with branches all over the Roman Empire. Well, first, he worked for somebody else's business, "for by trade they were tentmakers," refers to Priscilla and Acquilla. Just because Paul knew how to make tents doesn't mean that he made this his great preoccupation. Even while he was doing this, he was receiving financial aid from more than one church. "I robbed other churches by accepting support from them in order to serve you" (II Corinthians 11:8). He infers here that the Corinthian brethren should have been supporting him in preaching the gospel in Corinth. This support frees the missionary to get the job of gospel preaching and soul-saving done. To fill this free time with civilian pursuits, is a neglect of the missionary mission, and a sin against those who give such support in order that the gospel might be preached. I have not been flooded with offers, but I have had to turn down a number of jobs that would have interfered with the job Christ called me to do. Nor am I boasting about what I have done, for necessity is laid upon us to preach the gospel and save some. Furthermore, Paul did not let "tent making" interfere with his missionary work. "When Silas and Timothy arrived from Macedonia, Paul was occupied with preaching" (Acts 18:5). This is what we have been saying. The missionary's occupation is preaching. The canary's occupation is singing.

35. WHAT I LIKE ABOUT MISSIONARY LIFE

. . . thus making it my ambition to preach the gospel, not where Christ has already been named, lest I build on another man's foundation, but as it is written, "They shall see who have never been told of him, and they shall understand who have never heard of him." — ROMANS 15:20, 21

Pioneering with the gospel! This is the great thrill of missionary work. Starting from scratch, not building on another's foundation. Bringing souls to Christ who have never heard of Him before. Reaching people with the gospel who never had a chance before. Sharing to a little degree the ambition of the apostle Paul. This is the missionary spirit! This is the spirit of adventuring by faith!

What a great adventure it was for Christ to leave heaven and come to earth. What challenges to His soul! What a life of new and unforgettable experiences! How worthwhile it was! What happiness was brought to millions.

In missionary life, you go by faith into the unknown. You bet your life on the promises and providence of God. You are willing to take risks for the sake of the gospel. Away with the life of self-centered coddling! Away with the comforts of home! Away with the false security of this world, and forward into the real security of dependence upon God. This missionary pushes his frail bark into unknown seas. This fool of Christ risks all, yet gains all. What a joy to this happy pioneer to arrive in strange places, and find Christ is there. To find Christ in the happy eyes of those who obey the preached gospel. To teach songless hearts to sing, and see hopeless hearts begin to hope. To go where there is no church of Christ and see born before your very eyes the kingdom of God. This is what I like about missionary life.

To meet the challenges, to have every fiber of your soul and personality tested and tried. To be purified by the ups and downs, the successes and failures, the joy and sorrow. To be on the firing line where all the courage and ingenuity of your being is needed. To be in the place where victories are won against seeming overwhelming odds. What can take the place of experiences like this? To be where one is desperately needed. To be where the forces of unbelief and darkness are being rolled back by the armor of God. This is the missionary's life! Where else must all be committed to God? Where else does your life and work hang by a thread? Where else do you feel and need the grace of God so much, so often?

How can young men and young women keep still in the comfortable pews of the homeland? How can they resist the missionary call? How can the hearts of the mature fail to be moved by the challenge of world evangelism?

This is the life for me! I pray God will keep my feet to this fire. I pray Christ will put up with me on the firing line of foreign missions. I want only that He keep us where the action is! Where things are tough, where grace is great. Where things come hard, but they come of your own faith and work. Where you stand, not on another's foundation, but on the one you laid. Where you feed, not as a parasite upon the labors of others, but as one who treads the grain himself. This is what I like about missionary life.

36. WHAT I HATE ABOUT MISSIONARY LIFE

*In toil and hardship, through many a sleepless night.
. . . And apart from other things, there is the daily
pressure upon me of my anxiety for all the churches.*
— II CORINTHIANS 11:27-28

No one I know has been through hardships like our brother
Paul. But all missionaries share to some degree the pressures
and anxieties he faced. I would not want to give the impression
that Paul complained about his trouble, nor do I care to
complain, but there are times when problems and tensions will
lay you out either on your face or the flat of your back. "We
were so utterly, unbearably crushed that we despaired of life
itself" (II Corinthians 1:8).

We would not be honest if we didn't say there were certain
aspects of it that we hated. There is no use putting up a false
front by giving the impression that all is fine and dandy. I once
tried to counsel a new missionary about what to do when he
gets discouraged. He replied, "I never get discouraged." End of
counseling. Needless to say, he has since been discouraged more
than once.

One of the first hateful experiences of the missionary is loneliness. This is especially true of wives and children. It may be
a great adventure for the husband to be out among the people,
teaching and making friends. He feels a sense of accomplishment, but this is very different from the feeling of isolation and
loneliness with which the wife must battle. Then the time comes
when he runs out of gas. His zeal to get things done himself
may have robbed him of fellow-workers and companionship,
and the pressures and the loneliness combine to drop him in
his tracks. Sometimes the longer one stays on the field, the
lonelier he can get. I have seen my companions come and go.
It doesn't take long to become a veteran. But this means there
are few with whom we may talk shop. In a sense you must go
it alone.

There are times when there is a great influx of souls, and the
work seems to be making rapid progress. This is always encour-
aging. But most of the time it takes slow, steady plodding in

73

order to move ahead. It is this slowness, this seeming, never ending repetition of sameness. The brethren don't seem to be making any spiritual progress at all. The work is on a tread-mill. It looks like a waste of time. One step forward, two steps backward. Baptized a hundred, lose ninety. Get ten new members, lose ten old members. I hate this.

There is the uncertainty of what you are doing. Will it last? Will everything be for nought? Could I do better somewhere else? The missionary is nearly always a square peg in a round hole. The forces of paganism make holes in our ranks. Why do new programs soon run down? Like riding the waves, it is up and down, up and down. Just when things seem to be going so well, something·gets in the way, and things come to a grinding halt, and you have to .get started again. This is what I hate about missionary life.

If it wasn't for the promise of the Lord "in due season we shall reap," I'd chuck the whole business and get out from under the pressures. But we do all things for Christ's sake, for the one who loved us and died for us, and lives for us. By and by it will all be supremely worthwhile. We will be glad we stuck to it. We will be ashamed of our falterings, and will wish we had done more, and had done it longer. One second in Heaven should take care of anything we have put up with for our Lord.

37. MARRIED MISSIONARIES

Do we not have the right to be accompanied by a wife, as the other apostles and the brothers of the Lord and Cephas? — I CORINTHIANS 9:5

You can't get married like Peter and then expect to live like Paul. If you consider home responsibilities an interference with your work for Christ, then please don't get married. Our Lord grants the privilege of having a wife with you in the work of preaching the gospel. As you know, privilege and responsibility are twins. If you want a short, unhappy stint on the mission field, then take a wife with you and neglect her. Through neglect, some missionaries force their wives to compete with

Christ for their affection. This is wrong and cruel. A wife is not a burden, but a help-meet for you. In marriage she becomes your body. Now what happens to your body? It gets sick doesn't it? Well, this is what happens to some missionary wives. Their husbands make them sick. The result is they make their husbands sick. A sick marriage will not last under the pressures of missionary work, and while it does, it becomes a poor example, and a stumbling block to the work.

Marriage does circumscribe some activities of the missionary, but this must be accepted by the husband. To give your wife the impression that she is in the way, makes her feel unneeded and discouraged. She will then resent that which you have allowed to come between you, and this can even endanger her faith in Christ. You must take time, and make the effort necessary to have a stable, happy home. In the long run, this will be a tremendous blessing to the work. Marriage may interfere with some missionary activities but it definitely enhances others. A missionary with a happy home life, is going to be a happy missionary. A mess in your home will mean a mess in the churches where you are working. Your attitude, temper, and spiritual life depend on the unity and happiness maintained in your marriage. I have seen some missionaries subject their families to hardships that even the heathen around them would refuse to do. I guess they did it in the name of Christ, but I'm afraid it would have embarrassed our Lord. Necessary sacrifices can be justified to wife and children, but useless ones only breed discontent and disrespect. If you make your wife and children happy in the country where you are laboring, you will be happy also. If you fail in this, you will fail in the field, and it will mean an unhappy journey to the homeland.

Affection and consideration are not wasted on a wife. You can double the impact of your missionary effort when you have a wife backing you to the limit. You will accomplish more for the Lord if you have children who sympathize and back you in your work for Christ. To get their backing, you must win it, cultivate it. You must give your garden attention. Weed it from time to time, water it, and take pride in it. If you want your family behind missionary work, then make them a part of it.

Let them know what's going on. Give them something to do.

One way of ducking your family responsibilities, is to be away all the time. Live like a bachelor even if you are married. This is a good way to store up lots of heartbreak and frustration. One day the roof of your home will come down on your head. Certainly, for the work's sake, you must be away at times. This can be kindly explained and kindly accepted. Trips away will be accepted if you make yourself at home when you are home. Your love for being home will make you loved and missed when you are away from home. Sometimes you can take your wife with you. When you can, do it. You'll never regret it. The apostles and the brothers of the Lord were accompanied by their wives in their work for Christ and the church. Why not us?

38. FRIENDLINESS OR FAMILIARITY?

Just then his disciples came. They marveled that he was talking with a woman. . . . — JOHN 4:27
And when she was baptized with her household, she besought us saying, "If you have judged me to be faithful to the Lord, come to my house and stay." And she prevailed upon us. — ACTS 16:15

The native church was in a turmoil. Was the missionary having an affair or not? Wasn't the widow getting money from him? Wasn't he taking her home at night after meetings in his car? Fortunately, it was just gossip. Unfortunately, it hurt all concerned. Could it have been prevented? Maybe yes, maybe no, but there is one thing for sure, we can learn to be cautious.

Chances are an American missionary will find himself working in a society more conservative than the one he has left, especially in the social relationships of men and women. Friendliness can be taken as familiarity. Now, missionary friend, some of these nut-brown maidens are cute kids, but you had better leave them alone. You are already under suspicion because you are a free-wheeling American. Your friendliness will confirm in the minds of many your already questioned motives. Your influence can be ruined by too much attention to the women. Respectable families will not want their women attending your meetings, and enemies of Christianity will use it to blaspheme the good name of our Lord.

You must protect yourself, and yet protect those women who have a sincere interest in Christ. You do this by a sound sense of propriety and modesty. You need never be alone with a woman. Many a preacher has been stretched on the rack needlessly for lack of wisdom along these lines. The best answer to gossip is consistent prudence. The disciples were surprised to find Christ talking to a woman. Not that he didn't talk to women, but that it seems that it was His policy not to talk to women alone, and not to talk to strange women alone. There are exceptions to this rule, even as Christ's conversation with this Samaritan woman was exceptional conduct on His behalf. The foreign missionaries stayed at the home of Lydia, but she had to beseech them and persuade them of its appropriateness, for it was their policy not to behave as to give rise to damaging rumor. She convinced them of her own good motives and character, and thus they agreed.

American missionaries have given the impression that they are more interested in women than in men. They will go out of their way to do things for women that they would not do for men. In societies that are men-centered this gives Christianity the reputation of being effeminate. Men are repulsed by it, and missionaries find churches full of women. I am not a woman hater, but if we want leadership in the churches; if we want the gospel to be accepted in foreign societies, we must reach the men. Men wrote the New Testament, men lead the way in missionary work. Elders are men. Evangelists are men. Christ was a man. God is called "Father." The Holy Spirit is called "He." The man is head of the woman, and the woman is not to teach in church meetings, and is to be in subjection to the man. We must reach the women through the men, not the men through the women. In societies where husbands and wives show no affection in public, it is not appropriate for us to show interest in their wives, let alone their daughters. If you feel compelled to prove that you are a ladies' man, convince your wife at home. Be a man to your own woman. To single missionaries, I would say if you are doing personal evangelism with a woman, make sure your interest is only in her soul. As with some workers I have seen, you seem to be only interested in the souls of women. I'd advise a marriage for you, and more interest in the souls of men. Are you friendly and/or familiar?

39. DO YOU HAVE A DESERT HANDY?

And he saith unto them, "Come ye yourselves apart into a desert place, and rest awhile." — MARK 6:32

And he himself was in the stern, asleep on the cushion. — MARK 4:38

I knew I was right and everyone else was wrong. My fellow-workers were ganging up on me because they were unsound in their teaching, and sneaky in their personal relations. What were they doing on the mission field anyway? They wasted hours by visiting, playing games, going to the movies and what have you. They stood around telling jokes that weren't even funny, when there was work to be done!

Does the above sound familiar? Maybe a little like you? Needless to say, I was approaching a nervous breakdown. When you lose your sense of humor, look out! Good humor is a sign of good mental health. When you lose one you lose the other. I was exhausted. I had completed two years on the field and had run out of gas. As I lost my cool, my personal relations got hotter. There was no one around to tell us when to take a holiday, and I felt guilty when I wasn't working. But you can't leave your holidaying until furlough time. Furloughs are good for us, but are very busy times. God has given us our bodies to use, not abuse. We must listen to our bodies as well as to our consciences. When you start getting danger signals from within, you better slow down and take a look. I have learned not to be ashamed of taking a rest when I'm tired. You know, people in hot countries take siestas for more than one reason. We Temperate Zoners are quick to call someone lazy, and certainly there is such a thing as laziness; but at the same time climate, diet, etc. can determine how much you are capable of doing.

A friend of mine criticized Okinawan workers for sleeping on the job. Every day about eleven-thirty they would stretch out in the shade and sleep an hour. Well it was easy for this American who got up at nine to think those who had been up since six were tired and lazy. It is easy to look out of the window of an air-conditioned Temperate Zoned atmosphere and criticize those who live and work in the oppressive heat and humidity. It is too easy also, to belittle native preachers and workers as being lazy after we eat a well-balanced meal and compare it with the calory-deficient diets of some of them.

Now I don't think that we, with all of our twentieth-century contraptions to boot, are any better than the Lord and His disciples.

Day after busy day, thronged by crowds, and pressed by work, the disciples were tired. They needed to get away from the ever-demanding duties of their work and rest awhile. Laborers in the vineyard need rest in order to be well-balanced and faithful workers. To prodigally spend oneself in overwork is contrary to the self-control taught by the Spirit, and invites extreme reactions spiritually, mentally and physically. Christ was not a superman, and neither were the disciples. We can over-emphasize the work we must do, as if God were helpless and couldn't get along without us. When zeal oversteps itself and becomes anxious or proud, faith becomes unbelief, and our work becomes an idol. We not only need to see Jesus calming the stormy seas by the power of God, but we need to see Him sound asleep in the boat.

We must recognize the need to get away from work to rest awhile. The short-lived efforts of foreign missionaries, their nervous collapses, their distempers and resentments, can be traced many times, to their failure to recognize the need for proper rest and recreation. In missionary labors for the Lord there is a "desert place" to "rest awhile."

40. "ALL MISSIONARIES' CHILDREN ARE SPOILED BRATS"

See that you do not despise one of these little ones; for I tell you that in heaven their angels always behold the face of my father who is in heaven.

— MATTHEW 18:10

When I heard this my hackles began to rise, but when I considered the source I calmed down. After all, someone who has never attempted to raise one child doesn't really know an awful lot about the subject. I remembered also that before I had children I made similar statements thinking that I was an authority on the subject of raising children. After having had experience with a few kids, unfortunately, I have been forced to take the humble position of confessing my ignorance. I suspect though that I am not the only one.

Some of my colleagues have inferred in one way or another that missionaries' children are "kind of strange" and "different." Usually this is meant in some undesirable way. Well, let me tell you that the feeling is mutual. Maybe we could call it "mutual misery," because I get the same feeling when I'm around your children. I know people expect more from preachers' children, and are disappointed when they find out that they aren't any better than their own.

I read in one of our religious papers the other day, a news item about how well MK's were doing at a certain college. I found that MK meant "Missionary Kid." I'm sure it was a term of affection but it irritated me just the same. If I was an MK (and I'm glad I'm not) I could get along without that kind of affectionate terminology. Over here my children are called by some (who are not their friends) PK's, which stands for "Preacher's Kids." Of course, we could say CK's for "Church Kids," and I would be tempted to say TBK's for "The Brethren's Kids."

But let us restrain ourselves. I noticed that the article mentioned only those that were doing well, and left out those who were not in the top 10 per cent. Reports written by the brethren back home are just like those written by missionaries — they mention only the good stuff. As one who never made the top 10 per cent in college, I can appreciate the silence. I hope my children do better in school than I did, but I'm not going to take a fit if they don't. What gets me is, Why should anyone think it strange or newsworthy if some missionary's kids are smart, and also, Why should we be surprised or critical if some of them are not so smart? I expect that our "brats" are as good as your "brats," and your "brats" are as bad as our "brats."

We have visited in the homes of many Christians over there and over here and found problems with children about the same. Children are wonderful, and God loves every one of them, large and small. Children I know most about though are overseas and I want you to know that they are not "spoiled brats." They may be "spoiled" but they are not "brats," and they may be "brats," but they are not "spoiled." Sound contradictory? Well, children are like adults in this respect, but let us not despise the least of them.

Missionary children are tops with me. If they are a little "different" it could be for many reasons. Most of them have had the broadening experience of at least two cultures. They can speak two languages. They have been raised on the firing line where the gospel is being pioneered in conflict with pagan societies. They can learn to do without, or "take it" when the going gets rough. Along with their parents, they may bear scars for the sake of Christ; but before God this will be to their glory, and not to their shame.

Educating children on the field is probably the greatest single problem that married missionaries face. Most missionaries do not neglect their children and are trying their best under various circumstances. But the failure to find a satisfactory solution to children's education probably causes more missionaries to leave the field than anything else. Even so, educating children should not be our primary goal in life as missionaries. If that were the case, we should not have left home in the first place. Children must learn to share in the mission of their parents. If we teach them that their education is more important than preaching the gospel in the field that Christ has led us to, then will they not consider the work of Christ a hindrance to their progress, and a resented competitor of secondary importance? We are never going to educate our children properly for Christ unless we are fully dedicated ourselves. Children must learn in a happy way that they are not the center of the universe, and that the central purpose of the lives of the missionary parents is not the satisfying of their every whim. More than anything else, we want our children to be loyal servants of Christ; but they are not going to learn what this means by the half-starved, half-baked dedication of their parents. Therefore, we do not believe that missionary parents should be apologetic to their children for bringing them up overseas; and brethren back home should not give the child the idea he is deficient in some way if he has been overseas.

41. FIGHT WITH GOD ABOUT IT

I will not let you go, unless you bless me.
— GENESIS 23:26

"We have baptized thirty and only five or six attend faithfully. What can we do?" said the missionary's letter. Another read, "What plan can I use in my work? I am discouraged. Nothing seems to go right. How do I get started?" "Why is the work so slow?" These and other queries represent some of the struggles going on in the minds of missionaries. Sometimes the days get pitch black; there are fears within and without. We feel like we are on a treadmill going round and round, getting nowhere fast. Everything seems to be falling to pieces. We could wish that we had never left the homeland, and that any place must be better than the one we are in.

The fires of God's testing can rage pretty hot. No one can pass through them without getting singed. These are the times of our "Peniel," when we come "face to face" with God. Like Jacob, we must decide whether or not we are going to trust God's promise. Or whether or not we are going to lay all of our good and loved ones on the line for the Lord. It was easier for Jacob at Bethel, than at Peniel. At Bethel, when he had nothing, and had laid his head upon the stone pillow, God appeared to him and promised him everything. He was as a sinner who had nothing and was given everything. But now he has many possessions; he is facing death and total loss because of God's word. In the loneliness and darkness of the northern bank of the Jabbock, Haran must look pretty good to him now; and his selfish father-in-law, Laban must look very kind. In this place of fear and doubt, Jacob comes to grips with God's message and God's messenger. He grasps by faith and wrestles with the Lord all night. He seeks the promised blessing, and will not let go until he receives it. At this time, he becomes a true man of God. He is named Israel, Prince of God.

From this fight with God he receives a physical disability. He must limp the rest of his life; but every time he does, he is reminded not of defeat, but of victory, of facing God and surviving, of overcoming by the firm grasp of faith on the promise of God.

There is no way to avoid "Peniel." On the far-flung battleline all that Christ means to us is put to the test, and out of it God creates "Princes of Israel." The promise of Christ that all missionary workers hold dear is put to the test, "And lo, I am with you alway even unto the end of the world." Will we patiently labor with Christ? Will we see it through to the end? Are you with us Lord? Am I wasting my time? Will any good come of it? It is with God and with men that we have these struggles, and they are not one-sided. Jacob wrestled all night for a blessing. You know, as we struggle with God, God struggles with us. He asks us, "Do you really believe my promise? Are you going to turn back? Is personal security and comfort more important than the task I have given you? Do you love me most of all? Will you feed my sheep?" God seeks from us the strong affirmative by which we are blessed; justification by faith in His promises! We cannot be passive, or timid in this struggle if we hope to survive as a prince in God's household. The blessing comes through a fight to the finish. Facing God without fear, grasping Him with faith, expecting the reality of God's blessings.

Now, we cannot expect to go through battle without suffering and wounds. The resurrected body of Christ still bore the scars of the cross. The church, which is the newly created body of

Christ, cannot expect anything less than this. Those who give themselves to the work of the cross will come away bearing in their bodies the "marks of the Lord Jesus." They will limp away from the struggle, not in shame, but in victory, not as hirelings, but as shepherds who give their lives for the sheep, not as defeated, but as one who has overcome, not destroyed but as one who has overcome, not destroyed but as one who has come face to face with God and still lives. It is for this reason the missionary sticks to the job. It is for this that missionaries of Christ bear the toil, the sweat, and the heat of battle. It is for this that fevers and sickness, fears and indignities are borne. Let us not therefore, be afraid of the dark. Let us accept the challenge that God gives us. Let us exact the blessing from the struggle itself, and limp across the Jabbock as Israel, Prince of God.

42. WHY DON'T YOU ASK THEM?

I rejoice because I have perfect confidence in you.
— II Corinthians 7:16

There are no shortcuts in missionary work. I guess there are none in any kind of work that is done for the Lord. The people among whom we work have their own way of doing things and sometimes it seems that it is the slowest, most fouled-up way of doing things that the world has ever seen. Because of this, many times have I gone ahead planning things for others, controlling all and trusting none. Well it doesn't take long to find out that no one is following you, and worse than that, everyone seems to be opposing you. You're running too far ahead of the native Christians and they are discouraged by it. One of the descriptive terms early applied to me was translated "arbitrary." I have heard it used many times in describing other missionaries, too. A certain amount of stubbornness and confidence is all right, but when plans and decisions involve others they should be consulted. This is super-especially true when you are working in the unfamiliar situation of a country foreign to you.

I have spent many hours worrying about problems, trying to

decide what to do, imagining situations, trying to determine how the native Christians would react. I had studied a little psychology so I thought I could analyze and maneuver, maneuver and analyze. Well, finally I got enough sense to stop acting as if I knew everything, and start acting as if I needed help. When I wondered how my brethren felt about something I would ask them. When I was not sure of something, I would ask them about it. Pretty soon they got the idea that I was interested in them rather than just in pleasing myself. They enjoyed my ignorance and began to teach me many things. To my amazement I found out that they knew more about their people than I did! Not only that, but they also knew more about how to work in their own country than I did! How simple it all became!

A missionary's work is people. If people are not saved, if people do not grow up in Christ, if people do not become fellow-workers and stand on their own feet, what has a missionary to show for his labors? I don't do anything now without talking it over with my brethren. Sometimes it seems the most inefficient thing to do, but in the long run it bears the most fruit. Instead of taking responsibility for everything, we must share it with others. Only in this way will our brethren ever learn to carry on whether the missionary is present or not.

I have been asked the question "How do you get the natives to do their own work?" "Well, why don't you ask them?" I reply. Whether or not they are going to be good Christians is also their problem. They have got to worry about whether or not the church is going to make it financially. I believe the missionary's greatest responsibility along this line is the creating of an atmosphere for growth — a climate in which the native Christians can freely express themselves, and freely take upon themselves the responsibility of leadership. How do we create this atmosphere? First, we have to get off our high horses and admit our ignorance. Second, we have to learn to eat crow and like it. We need to find the Lord's way, and see that it is done. But the Lord's will and way is equally that of the new Christian's as it is ours. Missionaries do not have a monopoly on the wisdom and grace of God. If you think you are something, well, maybe you are, but as the old Oriental proverb says, "Even a monkey sometimes falls from a tree." A humble recognition of error, and an expression of confidence in the abilities of others will go a long way in creating a climate favorable to all kinds of spiritual growth. Not only that, but the deepest and most rewarding experiences come in close fellowship with other Christians. "The breadth and length and height, and depth" of the love of Christ is comprehended "with all the saints" (Ephesians 3:18). The love of Christ is understood through the sum total of the experiences of "all the saints." In fellowship with one another we probe the depths of the love of Christ. No one man has a monopoly on the knowledge and experience of the grace of Christ. No one Christian can comprehend it. It is comprehended together with others, learning from each other, completing in one another what is lacking in spiritual growth and understanding.

43. GASES, LIQUIDS, AND SOLIDS

Truly, I say to you, they have their reward.

MATTHEW 6:5

On the mission field, sometimes you wonder if anyone knows you're alive. Much that you do is not even appreciated by those with whom you are working. When the going is tough, every little gain seems of vast importance. Situations like this, coupled with the need to inform supporters about the work that is being carried on, can draw a missionary into a personal publicity campaign. When furlough time comes it seems that everyone must be informed about the wonderful work one is doing. When monies need to be raised, public relations problems arise. What kind of image does the work project? Are you known on the homefront? Are there pillars of the church "who will put you on the inside track? Angles are to be milked for all they are worth. When we are through with it all we can return to the field "well rewarded" for our endeavors. But I am afraid the Lord will agree saying, "Truly they have their reward."

Now, I consider public relations, publicity, "images," the repute of "pillars," etc., all gaseous in nature. Some of it may be harmless to be sure, but I doubt if the Lord has anything to do with it. Those who seem to be first in the work of the church may end up last, and they that seem to be last may end up first (Matthew 19:30). In other words, we live and work by the grace of Christ, and our reward will come by the same grace. If this reward is a gift what have we to boast about? Those who worked all day and those who worked only an hour received the same reward in the parable just referred to. And in Luke 13:23-30 those who were reputed to be the Lord's were not, and those who had no such reputation were the Lord's own. We can see therefore that our "image" could be of a very dubious nature, and a position granted by men could be unrecognized by our Lord.

Boasting, bragging, and all forms of self-exaltation are unreal, gaseous and without substance. To spend time and effort flailing around in a gas chamber is to invite judgment and death. If we reward ourselves and get others to reward us there will be no reward at the end of the line. "Every one who exalts himself will be humbled" (Luke 14:11). The application of the heat of self-importance to a good work can change that which was solid into that which is gaseous. Sometimes boasting starts without anything solid. It is gas all the way! Talking to my wife, I said, "We must be humble about what has been accomplished." She answered, "Has that much been accomplished that we need to be so humble?"

A man is what he is and not what he says he is. We are what we have actually done and not what people think we have done. We are what we actually do for the Lord, and not the position we hold in the church. It is possible to be called a missionary and not actually be one. You can be called a preacher and not preach much. You can be sent to save souls and not actually, personally, save one. You can have the reputation of a "spiritual giant" and actually be a midget. The great cloud of gas can obscure from vision the little accomplishment. A "position" can be occupied by a parasite who feeds on the accomplishment of others.

Now something solid and lasting comes from doing the will of the Lord from the bottom of your heart. It comes from seeking honor from God and not from men. It is happiness in what the grace of God accomplishes. It is satisfaction that comes from not doing righteousness before men to be seen of them. It is the deed done secretly that God rewards. It is the unknown, the last, that shall be first. The greatest of Christians is the one quietly living and working for the Lord. I am convinced that the humble servant hardly ever makes the headlines. It isn't necessarily necessary that he does. Headlines and newspapers are a recent invention anyway. Every man has only twenty-four hours in a day. You can only work to the limits of the health and ability God has given us. Can the "known one" put in more hours than the "unknown one." Will one receive more reward from the Lord because he has been given more abilities? I doubt it. "To whom much is given, of him will much be required" (Luke 12:48). But this does not make him any better than anyone else, and does not imply a greater reward. I believe that only God knows who the "pillars of the church" are. As we become known more among men, who can be known less by God. As we help ourselves to the rewards of our labors on earth, we empty the account of our rewards in heaven. As we enjoy reputation and prominence, that which was solid becomes liquid and runs away. It evaporates and becomes gaseous.

44. WILL YOU BURY YOUR BONES?

Feed my lambs. — JOHN 21:15

"*Hone wo uzumeru ka*" was the question that sent me to my Japanese-English dictionary. I knew that "*hone*" meant bone or bones, but I didn't know what "*uzumeru*" meant. Finally I saw that it meant "to bury." The Japanese Christians were asking me if I would "bury my bones in Japan." I replied that if I died in Japan I would probably be buried there. It would be too expensive to ship my body back home. This answer did not seem to satisfy them; in fact, they were telling me that I didn't even understand the question. Later I latched on to a Japanese brother who knew English and I asked him what they were driving at. He said, "They wanted to know what your intentions are as a missionary. The expression means total commitment to the people and the land you are working in. Are you willing to spend the rest of your life here? To live and die here with us?" "Now, I understand," was my reply. "Well, what about it?" the interpreter continued. "Are you?" "Well now, only God knows where my bones will be buried," I said. "No, you haven't understood yet. We Japanese want you to declare your intentions. We want to know whether we can trust you or not." The conversation was getting a little sticky for me, so I kept looking for a good way out of it. "The fellow is too insistent," I thought. "All right, you can trust me, I'll do my best. Thanks a lot. I'll see you later. *Sayonara*."

The next time I was asked that question I was better prepared to answer it. Also the next time, and the next time, and the next time. I guess every Japanese Christian I worked with asked me the same question. Some missionaries would have to answer "NO, I am only here for a couple of years and if I like it I might stay longer." Unfortunately, this may be an honest answer, but it certainly is not designed to win the affection of the nationals. They are not going to trust a "fly-by-night" proposition. It's kind of like trial marriage: if you like it you'll take it seriously; if you don't like it you'll back out. In the meantime though, children are born, and the wife and the children have the right to ask you to take care of them. Of course, I don't advocate trial marriage, or any kind of common law arrangement, but the feelings of newborn Christian nationals run along this line of thinking. Are you going to care for those who are born again under your ministry of the gospel? Are you a careless seed sower? You know, when you go "a courtin," the father has a right to ask if your intentions are honorable. He doesn't want you playing around with his daughter. Now, I know that you don't have to marry every girl you date, but you should prove that your intentions are good and proper.

Now it is obviously not God's will that missionaries always remain in one place, or even in one country. But it is just as obvious that Christ asks for unconditional commitment in those He calls to be fishers of men. After all of the sorrows and joys of the crucifixion and resurrection, the disciples went back to where they came from, and also back to what they came from. They went back to the fish business. They apparently still had their boats and nets available. Probably for "a rainy day." Anyway, there they were "selling insurance" or doing whatever they do when they "quit preaching" or "quit the field." But the Lord comes and recalls them saying, "Lovest thou me more than these [things]?" It is neuter, you Greek students. Christ was asking them for full time dedication to a full time work. According to some, He should have praised them for "making tents," but the Lord had more important things for them to do. Maybe He should have put them on "partial support" and let them continue with their fishing industry, gradually eliminating their preaching responsibilities so that they could be entirely self-supporting. Or if that was unacceptable, fix it so that they could serve the church on weekends only. You see, fishing on Galilee would be all right if their love is focused on the right thing. It would be all right if their hearts were set on the salvation of souls. It was all right for Paul to make tents as long as his "intentions were honorable," as long as it was done for the preaching of the gospel, for "woe was unto him" if he didn't preach it. You see, leaving a field of work is all right if it's in the area of your total dedication to Christ and Christians. Any "burying your bones in a country is acceptable only when your intentions are honorable.

Where will we actually bury our bones? As I once answered, "only God knows." But let us missionaries not miss the point of our brother's query. Are we willing to live and die in the land that Christ had led us to? Are we willing to go down the same road of life our native brethren go down? Are we willing to be worthy of their trust? This is the issue every evangelist of Christ must face. This is an issue for missionaries only. How about it? Where are you going to lay your bones to rest?

45. HOW TO MULTIPLY

But we will devote ourselves to prayer and to the ministry of the word. . . . And the word of God increased; and the number of the disciples multiplied greatly. . . . — ACTS 6:4, 7

I wish I had back all the time spent on this, that, and the other. In the normal course of events a missionary spends a lot of time just living. It takes at least twice as long to get something done in a foreign country than it does back home.

Now if you add to this all kinds of good works and generous services, you can be sure that not much time will be left for preaching.

This is what happened to the first missionaries as they worked together in the large congregation at Jerusalem. The physical needs of the new Christians demanded their attention to the extent that they found themselves faced with the decision as to whether or not they should "give up preaching the word of God to serve tables." They definitely refused to do this, remembering, I'm sure, their original commission and the example of the Lord.

Most missionaries I know about received their support to go to a mission field by appealing to their fellow Christians on the basis of what the Great Commission commands. The Commission says "preach," "teach." This is what we were sent to do, but somewhere along the line, a lot of us got off this track and ended up doing every other kind of task imaginable.

When the apostles relieved themselves of the tasks of waiting on tables and organized the work so that they could devote themselves to prayer and preaching, the "number of the disciples multiplied greatly." The key to church growth is found here. When the preaching of the Word of God increases, the number of the disciples increase. It is true that the growth of the church differs from place to place, and country to country, but the basic means that produces growth is the same. "Faith comes by hearing the word of Christ, and how can they hear without a preacher?" (Romans 10:17, 14).

My missionary colleagues, I think it would be a good idea for you to sit down and count the time you spend on preaching and keep a continual record of it. Let us make sure we are on the ball. Sometimes the work seems slow and difficult, and the church doesn't grow because we are not doing what it takes to multiply disciples.

Notice the apostles' refusal to be distracted. Notice their devotion to duty. A missionary who can't say No will not do much preaching. He will not save many souls. Too many distractions will soon have him off doing something else. I know there are vocational type missionaries giving their time to various good and splendid works, but I'm talking about we missionaries who came out under the Great Commission, and are expected by those who sent us to fulfill this Commission. As we complain about workers in the field being few and far between, are we planting, watering and reaping or are we back at the house doing tasks others could do, forever getting ready to go out and preach and never quite making it? It takes devotion to duty. We must continually offer ourselves to the work of preaching. Increased preaching will increase the Word, and increase the disciples.

Notice also that prayer precedes preaching. Prayerful preaching! Not just preaching, but preaching in spirit and in truth. Prayer will lead us to souls. Prayer will keep us doing what the Lord wants us to do, where he wants us to do it. Let us pray and then preach, preach and then pray, and thus follow the sterling example of the apostles, those first missionaries of the gospel who were led to fulfill the Great Commission of their Lord.

46. COULDN'T YOU GO BACK SOONER?

What then is to be done? They will certainly hear that you have come. — ACTS 21:22

It irritates me every time I recall what that elder said, but time has made me understand it a little. We were on our first furlough after five and a quarter tough years in Japan. The first are the worst. We were looking forward to taking it easy for awhile, and I wanted to go back to school and study more. But this elder had his problems too. Our presence had created a few for him and the quickest way out seemed to him to be our speedy return to Japan.

Sometimes we are so wrapped up in our own needs and problems that we missionaries fail to appreciate the trouble we cause others. The day after Paul arrived in Jerusalem, he was confronted with the problem that his presence brought the church there. When the Jews would hear that Paul had come, then all of the criticisms and false rumors would come to the fore and it could mean a lot of trouble for the church. Although the nature of Paul's problems and the ones that may arise when we return may be widely different, still there are things we need to be conscious of. We may need to straighten out false impressions.

More than once, returning missionaries have been asked to take certain stands on issues they knew very little about. More than once they have goofed and caused some concern in the home church. Communications are such today that missionaries can stay abreast of what develops in the church back home.

Sometimes the presence of a missionary makes it hard on the local preacher. Some Christians think missionaries are such saints that they glamorize them to the extent that the local man looks pretty poor in comparison. The missionary is also used as a club by the ever-present preacher critics, and it is with a great sigh of relief that the local preacher sees him on his way. These things should not be, but unfortunately these do happen. There is no caste system in the church, but when it comes to missionaries and the way some unrealistic church members view them, they are placed in the category of "untouchables." Such a view of missionaries is not really good for them, for it hinders them when they try to give an honest picture of the work to supporters. It prevents very warm relations between themselves and those to whom they are responsible.

Every church has its problems and some of them have to be treated with great finesse. Just as the local man has managed this art in the congregation he is working for, the bungling missionary returns and ignorantly upsets the apple cart! We do not need to be free with advice until we know what we are talking about. We must be sympathetic with the situations into which we enter and be careful not to leave a mess behind us.

Again, I have sat in some audiences and listened to some missionaries talk me into feeling ashamed of being a missionary. They brow-beat the audience, made themselves superior and every one else inferior. They were after money and were trying to make everybody feel guilty enough to let go of a fair size of it. They may have received it once at that church, but I doubt if they would ever get it again. These missionaries leave behind resentment at being manipulated. Their blustering, belittling attitude left behind a lot of problems for the local men, and for missionaries who might come after them.

I must admit that I have come back from the field and approached churches with some feelings of resentment. Resentment of their failure to understand and back the work as they should. Resentment of their smug, self-centered ways. But there's a shoe that fits the other foot too. Christians at home can resent the failure of missionaries to understand and back the work on the home front. They can resent the smug, self-centered ways of the missionary money raiser.

Now, if we are going to be fellow-workers for Christ, we must learn to get along. We must be sympathetic of each other's needs and problems, and like Paul, be willing to accept the advice of other Christians and do those things which will put down false impressions, and lead to mutual understanding, removing any stumbling blocks that may be in the way.

47. HOW OLD SHOULD A MISSIONARY BE?

So we do not lose heart though our outer nature is wasting away, our inner nature is being renewed every day. — 1 CORINTHIANS 4:16

Many times I have heard the sad moan, "I wish I had become a missionary," and, "If I was younger I would do what you are doing," plus, "If I were your age I'd go into the mission field." The older I get, the less I hear that last one, because most of the moaners are pretty close to my age.

Granting that there are Christians who really feel that way, it is still hard for me to believe them. I figure that a soul-winner for Jesus is busy doing that and is already involved in "missionary work." I reckon that they have had plenty of opportunities to make decisions about doing missionary work. Most of the few missionaries we support have to scrounge around all over the country to find adequate help, so there are few places they miss. There are few congregations that have not been challenged concerning the fulfillment of the Great Commission in some way or other. Those who are dreaming of some future day when they will give themselves to the work of Christ have already missed the boat! If you are not a light where you are, a change in geography will not make you one. Only a change in heart will do that. Those who are going into full time evangelism when they retire and are not busy at it now are talking through their hats. If you are busy at soul winning now, I can believe that you will be busy at it in the future also. Men become evangelists not by ordination, not by graduation, but by evangelization. If you really want to become a missionary, then start missionizing. Find out from God what His mission for you is and start working at it.

How old do you have to be? Ask the eighty-year-old Moses, and the twelve-year-old Josiah. Try the fifty-year-old Paul, or the twenty-year-old Timothy. The Lord placed no age limits on those He called to do His work. Age might determine the type and quality of the work that God wants done, but God wants all Christians, old and young, to become involved in missionary work.

How old do you have to be? We might better ask, "How young can you be?" It might be better to get off to an early start. I celebrated my 21st birthday on the boat to Japan. But I have met some teen-agers with the mental outlook of an old fuddy duddy, and some senior citizens as young and fresh in mind and heart as anyone could be. I'm convinced that there are too many preparing for comfortable retirement who ought to be preparing for missionary work. We have too many heading for Senior Citizens Homes that ought to be heading for mission fields. You might as well suffer rheumatism in India as in Indiana. Your retirement money would be better spent on the living church of God, than on a dead body. We have seen our "young" sixty-and seventy-year-olds pioneering the gospel in India, Korea, and Japan. Also Uncle Sam has scattered Christians of all ages here and there throughout the whole world. I have seen older brethren take assignments in foreign countries in order to make money. Why can't they do it in order to save souls? If men and women will go overseas and suffer hardship, pain and death out of duty for their country, why can't we do it [illegible] too late to serve the Lord, but we must start now. Not tomorrow, not after retirement, not after it becomes more convenient, but right now. How old should a missionary be? You tell me. Better still, you tell the Lord.